GOD
AND
HAMILTON

SPIRITUAL THEMES FROM
THE LIFE OF ALEXANDER HAMILTON
&
THE BROADWAY MUSICAL
HE INSPIRED

by
KEVIN CLOUD

God and Hamilton: Spiritual Themes from the Life of Alexander Hamilton & the Broadway Musical He Inspired
© 2018 by Kevin Cloud

Published by Deep River Books
Sisters, Oregon
www.deepriverbooks.com

ISBN—13: 9781632694775

Cover Photo of the Author © Daniel Williams

Library of Congress: 2018933921

Printed in the USA
2018—First Edition

10 9 8 7 6 5 4 3 2 1

Cover design by Jeremy Shellhorn

Praise for *God and Hamilton*

"Cloud's Christlike compassion turned me inside out and revealed a side of Hamilton I had never thought to explore."

— LAUREN BOYD,
HAMILTON BROADWAY CAST

"In this book Kevin portrays a wonderful example of how you can draw from contemporary culture to understand how God works with us on our own heroic journeys. I found his emphasis on God's grace and faithfulness particularly inspiring and think that all who read it will come away with a better understanding of the challenges we all face. I cannot recommend it more highly!"

— MIKE BREEN,
FOUNDER OF 3DM,
AUTHOR OF *BUILDING A DISCIPLING
CULTURE, COVENANT AND KINGDOM,*
AND *FAMILY ON MISSION*

"A bold and creative exploration of the themes in life that matter most. If we have the eyes to see and the ears to hear, we will notice God everywhere. In this beautiful book, Cloud helps us see, listen, and open to the all-consuming love God pours out to us."

— PHILEENA HEUERTZ,
AUTHOR OF *PILGRIMAGE OF A SOUL:*
CONTEMPLATIVE SPIRITUALITY
FOR THE ACTIVE LIFE AND FOUNDING
PARTNER, GRAVITY, A CENTER FOR
CONTEMPLATIVE ACTIVISM

"How did Alexander Hamilton overcome a tragic and shame-filled childhood? Kevin Cloud celebrates the amazing grace that propelled Hamilton to become a key architect of our fledgling democracy. For all who struggle with doubt, depression, and despair, *God and Hamilton* offers an inspiring way forward. Kevin Cloud's book made my heart sing!"

— CRAIG DETWEILER,
PRESIDENT, THE SEATTLE SCHOOL
OF THEOLOGY AND PSYCHOLOGY

"C. S. Lewis once lamented that people too often fail to appreciate the real and serious glory of even the most dull and uninteresting human life; that if we could ever truly glimpse the beauty of a normal everyday person's story we might actually be tempted to worship them. In *God and Hamilton*, Kevin Cloud offers precisely this kind of appreciative glimpse into the life of Alexander Hamilton. These pastoral reflections upon a life that was anything but dull and uninteresting are sure to inspire.

Read this book and catch a new imagination for what it means to be human."

— TIM SUTTLE,
PASTOR AND AUTHOR OF *SHRINK:*
FAITHFUL MINISTRY IN
A CHURCH-GROWTH CULTURE

"Eliza Hamilton's commitment to the children of her day was born out of her love for an orphan who changed the course of our nation, and was shaped by her abiding faith. We at Graham are inspired by Eliza's conviction, strength of character, and loving spirit as we continue to lead the organization she co-founded to care for children growing up in conditions her husband, Alexander, would have found familiar. Kevin Cloud beautifully captures this powerful story that is inspiring the world."

— JESS DANNHAUSER,
PRESIDENT AND CEO
OF GRAHAM WINDHAM

"You'd have to be living under a rock not to know about the Broadway play *Hamilton*. It's developed an enormous following. I didn't really know all the spiritual implications of Hamilton's life though until I read Kevin's book. My appreciation grew for the musical, but mostly for Hamilton. What a great read!"

— RON EDMONDSON,
PASTOR AND AUTHOR OF
THE MYTHICAL LEADER

Kevin Cloud has masterfully tapped into the resurgent interest in Alexander Hamilton by crafting a captivating, wholly entertaining, and spiritually insightful book. As a talented, multi-faceted, and gifted visionary, Hamilton continues to connect with our modern society in a unique way. His principled words and actions have long been associated with spiritual guidance. Cloud takes his reader on a fascinating journey, connecting those inspired dots of Hamilton's life, and marries them with our perception of God in our culture. In doing so, he provides powerful, transformative lessons and tools for our times. A fun and purposeful read indeed.

— DR. GREGORY JANTZ,
AUTHOR OF *TURNING YOUR DOWN INTO UP*

"*Hamilton* is more than just a musical and has the power to change lives, and in *God and Hamilton* author Kevin Cloud illuminates why a Broadway show affects so many of us deeply and on such a personal level. Kevin skillfully weaves insights about the musical, Alexander Hamilton's life, and his own experiences and spiritual guidance into a tapestry that not only illustrates the amazing work that Lin-Manuel Miranda created but that also makes you reexamine the life you're leading. Entertaining and thought-provoking, *God and Hamilton* is a compelling read whether or not you've seen the show."

— BRYAN BARRERAS,
AUTHOR OF *WHERE WAS THE ROOM WHERE IT HAPPENED?: THE UNOFFICIAL HAMILTON— AN AMERICAN MUSICAL LOCATION GUIDE*

"With a pastor's heart and a mind at work, Kevin Cloud unearths novel and crucial insights at the intersection of Alexander Hamilton's life and our own. He has also done his homework, grounding his claims in the rich context of the revolutionary era."

— T. J. TOMLIN,
ASSOCIATE PROFESSOR OF HISTORY,
UNIVERSITY OF NORTHERN
COLORADO AND AUTHOR OF
A DIVINITY FOR ALL PERSUASIONS

"This book is a testament to how God can use the arts to transform us. With the heart of a true pastor, Kevin Cloud masterfully weaves together historical details from the lives of Hamilton and his contemporaries, scenes from Lin-Manuel Miranda's beautiful musical, and contemporary stories of faith. In these pages, Cloud moves easily among the roles of theologian and storyteller, pastor and friend. I loved this book, and think that anyone who has found his or her imagination captured by the life story of Alexander Hamilton will enjoy the way Cloud examines these experiences in light of the stories of the Bible—from the Psalms to the Gospels to the Revelation."

— KATIE SAVAGE,
AUTHOR OF *GRACE IN THE MAYBE:
INSTRUCTIONS ON NOT KNOWING
EVERYTHING ABOUT GOD*

"Kevin doesn't take the safe road in life. He jumps in the middle of one of the biggest phenomena in Broadway theater history, *Hamilton*. Kevin jumps head first into this intersection of music and history. He unearths rich and livable connections with Biblical truth. When was the last time you read a book that made you want to see a Broadway show and read the Bible? Kevin manages to do both as he traverses the fascinating textures of both the musical and history about Alexander Hamilton and his relationship with God."

— ROY MORAN,
AUTHOR OF *SPENT MATCHES*

Table of Contents

Acknowledgments

I will never forget the moment I walked out of the Richard Rogers Theatre after seeing *Hamilton* on Broadway. Although I couldn't articulate it at the time, I knew I had experienced a deeply spiritual work of art. Thank you, Lin-Manuel Miranda, and the entire *Hamilton* team, for offering such a beautiful gift to the world.

The concept for this book developed after reading *Alexander Hamilton* by Ron Chernow, which was another gift to me. The majority of Hamilton's historical background in this book comes from Chernow's biography. Thank you to Ron Chernow, for your powerful book that cemented my obsession with all things Hamilton.

Thanks to Bill Carmichael, Carl Simmons, and the team at Deep River Books. You believed in this manuscript before anyone else did.

T. J. Tomlin: My bean boy, your friendship has been one of the true gifts in my life. I'll always be grateful for your wisdom, loyalty, unconditional love, and your ability to make me laugh.

Jim Gum: You have walked with me more patiently and with more wisdom than anyone else over the years. Whenever we spend time together, I leave a better person.

To so many other friends: Isaac Anderson, for your investment in my writing; to Jeremy Shellhorn for your generosity and ridiculous gift in design; to Craig Babb for your ongoing wisdom and direction.

To the Midwest Fellowship staff: I'm forever thankful for your friendship and partnership in the gospel. To Midwest Fellowship: Being your pastor is one of the great treasures of my life. I love chasing after the vision God has called us to together.

To countless others who have loved me and invested in my life, I am so thankful.

To everyone who helped make this book a reality: Rachelle Gardner for your ongoing wisdom, coaching, and encouragement. To Lindsey Crittenden for improving the manuscript in so many ways. To Kristen McClain, Janette Larison, and Donna Martin for all the edits and ideas. To Rand Scholet and Byran Barreras, for your insights and suggestions. To Harry Berberian and Jess Danhauser at Graham Windham: You guys are doing amazing work.

To my family, Mom and Dad, Steve and Micki, Matt and Stacey, Jeff and Kayce, and the Doubleday crew: What a blessing to have such a kind and loving family. As Dad always says, I'm thankful that we all actually like each other.

To my boys, Samuel, Benjamin, Andrew, and Levi: The four of you bring me more joy and pride than you could possibly imagine. I count it one of the great blessings of my life to be your father and to watch you grow up into the men God created you to be. You each are so unique, so wonderfully made, and you each make me so proud. I love you more than you will ever know.

And lastly, to Allison: What could I possibly say that would adequately capture how much you mean to me? How much I love you? How filled with gratitude I am whenever I think of our life together? If only I could write poetry as beautifully as you do. Since I can't, all I can think to say is that I love you, I cherish our relationship more than anything in this world, and I am eternally grateful that God allowed me to walk the face of this earth with you by my side. You have sacrificed so much so that I could follow my calling. Now it's your turn, and I have so much anticipation for this next season of life, where your voice rings out for the world to hear.

Introduction

Our collective cultural ignorance about Alexander Hamilton—his biography and his role in the formation of the American republic—began to transform into a cultural obsession in August of 2015. That month, Lin-Manuel Miranda's musical about Hamilton's life opened on Broadway, and became a cultural phenomenon like no other musical had before. People are paying thousands of dollars to secure tickets to the show. *Hamilton* has appeared on the cover of every major entertainment magazine. The cast recording rocketed up the Billboard charts, setting numerous records. Gyms across the country are offering *Hamilton*-themed workouts. The musical's popularity even influenced the US Treasury Department, which reversed a decision to replace Hamilton on the $10 bill. Hamiltonmania took over the country, and as of summer 2018 it hasn't showed signs of slowing down. *Hamilton* producer Jeffery Seller says, "I have never in my life witnessed a musical that has penetrated the American culture faster than *Hamilton*."

How is it that this musical, this story, this life, has so captured our culture's imagination? What is it about our cultural context that has created the soil for this story to take root and grow into such an unprecedented phenomenon?

* * *

One answer to these questions could be that the show is simply *that good*. *Hamilton* won eleven Tony Awards in 2016, including best musical, and was awarded the Pulitzer Prize for drama.

I saw *Hamilton* on Broadway with my wife in October of 2016. We settled into our seats and sensed a palpable excitement and anticipation in the theatre. The next two hours and forty-five minutes gripped us with its musical creativity, stunning lyricism, and emotional storytelling. I graduated with a music degree in college and have always appreciated musicals, but something about this production felt unlike anything I had ever witnessed.

The innovative show integrates rap and hip-hop on Broadway. Jeremy McCarter, a collaborator with Miranda on the musical and coauthor of *Hamilton the Revolution*, writes about how Miranda was the first writer to make this leap. Miranda used hip-hop "as form, not content. . . . [Hip-hop] is, at bottom, the music of ambition, the soundtrack of defiance." Although risky and unprecedented on Broadway, hip-hop provided the perfect genre for a musical about the American Revolution and the life of Hamilton.

The lyrics and music composition are genius. "You have no idea how lyrically amazing this show is from a rap perspective," gushes performance artist Lemon Anderson. In one of my favorite lyrics, Hamilton raps about his life's mission: forming a strong central government to unify the newly formed United States. In the lyric, Miranda brilliantly rhymes the words "democracy,"

"Socrates," "rocks at these," and "mediocrities." The meter and rhyme of his lyrics are fresh, insightful, and imaginative.

Seeing *Hamilton* was an unforgettable experience. I wept through a number of scenes, and left the theatre inspired and challenged. I agree with Michelle Obama's assessment of the show, who declared it "the best piece of art in any form that I have ever seen in my life."

* * *

Also, Hamilton's story intersects with a number of important social issues of our time, such as immigration, gender equality, and diversity. Hamilton himself was an immigrant from the Caribbean—a major theme drawn out through the entire story. Miranda calls it "the quintessential immigrant story, of redefining yourself when you come to a new place."

Central roles are given to women, who declare their equality throughout the production. Angelica Schuyler, Hamilton's sister-in-law, sings about Jefferson's Declaration of Independence and advocates for the inclusion of women in his famous opening line, "All *men* are created equal." Miranda rightly portrays Eliza, Alexander's wife, as a strong, intelligent, and kind woman, who deeply impacted the early republic alongside her husband. Hamilton's story simply could not be told without Eliza at the center of it.

Set in an era of slavery, questions of race are never far from the surface. Actors of color play the roles of the Founding Fathers, a casting decision that turns expectations upside down and challenges the audience to open itself up to new possibilities.

Christopher Jackson, who played George Washington in the original Broadway cast, says, "By having a multicultural cast, it gives us, as actors of color, the chance to provide an additional context just by our presence onstage, filling these characters up."

Cast members of *Hamilton* have made clear the importance of these issues in our cultural, and even political, conversation; on the night Vice President-elect Mike Pence attended the show, the cast spoke from the stage to implore the incoming administration to uphold the inalienable rights of all people. During the 2017 Super Bowl pregame show, three *Hamilton* actresses added the words, "and sisterhood" to the song "America the Beautiful." Surely, in part, *Hamilton* resonates with our culture because of the relevant social issues it raises. McCarter writes, "Sometimes the right person tells the right story at the right moment, and through a combination of luck and design, a creative expression gains new force. Spark, tinder, breeze."

* * *

Another, even deeper, explanation exists for the emergence of *Hamilton* as a cultural phenomenon. This show, and the story it tells, becomes a moment of spiritual transcendence for the people lucky enough to experience it. The night I saw the show I found myself unexpectedly drawn into the presence of God.

An act of grace initiates the story, enabling Hamilton to travel to New York and create a new life for himself. Hamilton receives forgiveness and unconditional love from his wife, Eliza. The play ends with one of the most powerful visual expressions of redemption I've ever witnessed. This musical teems with these moments of transcendence—moments where a powerful scene occurs on stage, and the entire atmosphere changes in the theatre. The audience collectively feels a weight, a tension, a presence, perhaps even the presence of God.

These moments, and others like them, led me into a recognition and remembrance of God's presence and activity in Hamilton's story, and in my story as well. I have to agree with Rosie O'Donnell, who, after seeing *Hamilton* more than fifteen times, described it as "a religious experience, a spiritual cleansing in a way. . . . *Hamilton* is medicine that I need for my soul. It is vital to me; it feels like going to church." After seeing a performance of *Hamilton*, she tweeted a picture backstage with the cast and added the hashtag #broadway #church.

I wonder if some have encountered the presence of God during *Hamilton* without fully recognizing it. John Guare, a playwright, saw a *Hamilton* workshop before it opened. He commented, "I haven't felt this alive in a show since I don't know when. You had that incredible feeling of when a door opens up and a brand-new wind blows through."

Feeling fully alive? Experiencing a new wind blowing through?

Sounds like the reality and presence of God to me.

For two hours and forty-five minutes, an ordinary Broadway theatre became for me a transcendent experience, a portal into the holy. Like the oversized wardrobe in C. S. Lewis' classic tale, *Hamilton* ushered me into an alternate reality, a reality that too often remains hidden in our day-to-day lives. This musical, and this story, draws people into the very presence of God and his kingdom among us. It has become and continues to be a "thin place" for me, and for so many others who have been impacted by this deeply spiritual work of art.

* * *

The language of "thin places" originated in ancient Celtic spirituality. The Celts believed that heaven and earth were not two faraway realities, but rather overlapped and intertwined. Heaven wasn't somewhere far away and almost unreachable, but here among us, with those who had eyes to see. The Celts believed that a veil somehow separated heaven and earth that kept us from clearly seeing this reality. But at these thin places, the veil became nearly translucent, and God became almost visible, tangible.

This way of thinking about heaven and earth is central to the Christian story. In his book *Simply Christian*, New Testament scholar N. T. Wright observes that heaven and earth "overlap and interlock in a number of different ways. . . . The Old Testament insists that God belongs in heaven and we on earth. Yet it shows over and over again that the two spheres do indeed overlap, so that God makes his presence known, seen, and heard within the sphere of earth. . . . (Jesus) is, at the moment, present with us, but hidden behind that invisible veil which keeps heaven and earth apart, and which we pierce in those moments . . . when the veil seems particularly thin."

Author and pastor Eugene Peterson agrees, "Heaven . . . is a metaphor that tells us that there is far more here than meets the eye. Beyond and through what we see there is that which we cannot see, and which is, wondrously, not 'out there' but right here before us and among us: *God*—his rule, his love, his judgment, his salvation, his mercy, his grace, his healing, his wisdom." God and his kingdom do not, in other words, reside in a faraway place up in the sky, but right here among us. What we need is a little peek behind, or through, the veil from time to time. We need to experience thin places to remind us of God's presence among us.

* * *

Hamilton marks only one of the many times I've experienced these thin places—places where God seems to break through, and what normally feels hidden becomes real and tangible. In these moments, I catch a glimpse of who I want to be and what it means to find real life, eternal life. I remember in these moments the truth that my life finds completion in God, and in God alone.

I am desperate for these reminders. Without them, I forget about God and who God calls me to be. I forget, so quickly, even naturally, about the life that I want to live, but seem incapable of. I forget about what makes my life meaningful and fulfilling. When I lose sight of these truths, I turn into a shadow of myself, becoming selfish, greedy, lustful, and proud. Thin places remind me that God is with me and knows the best path for my life. I need these reminders as much as my lungs need oxygen.

Art holds a unique power to usher us into a thin place, perhaps because of God's creative nature. Being made in the image of God, as all of us are, means we all have creative potential. When we experience the wonder and beauty of the creative act, perhaps we see what God saw at the very beginning, that this world is good. "God saw all that he made," the book of Genesis tells us, "and it was very good." Wright observes, "The arts are not the pretty but irrelevant bits around the border of reality. They are highways into the center of a reality which cannot be glimpsed, let alone grasped any other way." There is something about art that ushers us into the reality that is too often hidden and forgotten: the reality of God's presence among us. Art communicates, stirs emotions, and awakens us in ways that no other medium can.

The artist herself plays a central role in ushering us into these thin places, this hidden world where God reveals himself. There are moments, says author Fredrick Buechner, where "Shakespeare turns preacher," moments where Shakespeare's writing reveals truth to us in such a way that we experience transcendence and the veil becomes thin. Moments where we encounter the very presence, wisdom, and love of God. Author Madeleine L'Engle agrees, "And Shakespeare and all the other dramatists before and after him! Are they not revealers of truth?" If Buechner and L'Engle are right, if Shakespeare can turn preacher, is it possible that Miranda has done so as well?

Oskar Eustis, a collaborator on *Hamilton* and the artistic director of the Public Theatre, where *Hamilton* played before it opened on Broadway, agrees that Miranda is the Shakespeare of our time. He says, "I have more than once compared Lin to Shakespeare, and I do it without blushing or apologizing. Lin in *Hamilton* is doing exactly what Shakespeare did in his history plays. He is taking the voice of the common people, elevating it to poetry, and by elevating it to poetry ennobling the people themselves."

I believe that in the musical *Hamilton*, Miranda has turned preacher, or perhaps prophet. The story he tells about the life of Hamilton reverberates with the central truths of the Christian Scriptures. It becomes a thin place for us, reminding us of the presence of God among us. It points us toward love, grace, and redemption, and inspires us to transform our lives as a response to this transcendent experience.

* * *

There is an additional reason that *Hamilton* becomes a thin place, besides simply being great art. It becomes a thin place because Alexander Hamilton's story is deeply spiritual. My fascination with Hamilton and understanding of the spiritual themes of his life grew after I read Ron Chernow's biography of Hamilton, the book that inspired Miranda's musical.

The story of Hamilton's life is remarkable. He was born into destitute poverty in the Caribbean, and raised by parents living together in a common-law marriage. The circumstances of his birth fated Hamilton to live with the shame and stigma of illegitimacy throughout his life. When he was a young boy, a hurricane decimated the Island of St. Croix where Hamilton lived. An intelligent and articulate young man, he wrote a letter about the experience that was subsequently published by a local newspaper. Many who read it saw incredible potential in this young man, and raised money to send him to America to get an education. He arrived during the incubation of the American Revolution.

In America, he exhibited an uncanny knack for finding himself in the right place at the right time. He studied at King's College for a few years, but soon joined the revolution. He quickly caught the attention of George Washington as an effective artillery captain. Washington invited Hamilton to join his staff, and in a remarkably short amount of time, Hamilton basically served as Washington's chief of staff for the entire Continental Army. Hamilton played a crucial role in the Americans' victory over the British, including his central role leading the battle of Yorktown. During his time in the Army, Hamilton also met his future wife, Eliza Schuyler, who would prove to be one of the greatest blessings of his life.

After the war, Hamilton served, at Washington's invitation, as the first Secretary of the Treasury. This position gave him unprecedented opportunity to form and shape the new republic. He quickly became the second most powerful man in the young country, next to Washington. His impact on the early republic cannot be overstated. He "created the institutional scaffolding for America's future emergence as a great power . . . and helped weld the states irreversibly into one nation," writes Chernow. Henry Cabot Lodge, a Republican senator in the early 1900s, wrote, "We look in vain for a man who, in an equal space of time, has produced such direct and lasting effects upon our institutions and history."

Hamilton served as secretary for six years, and then resigned to practice law, primarily to improve his financial situation. He still enjoyed influence with George Washington, who consulted Hamilton often. A year later, Washington declined to run for a third term as president. Hamilton had lost his greatest advocate and friend in the new government, and proceeded to alienate almost every other Founding Father. He and the next president, John Adams, despised each other. Four years later, when his political rival Thomas Jefferson was elected president, Hamilton found himself without any significant government influence or official position. In only a few short years, he had fallen from a position of the highest possible influence to political exile. His descent was as shocking and swift as his rise to power. His life came to a sudden and tragic end at the age of forty-seven when a political opponent, Aaron Burr, shot and killed him during a duel of honor between the two men.

Behind these historical details, a deeply spiritual story emerges. Hamilton's life tells a story of authentic faith, love, grace, and forgiveness. We also see a story of shame and regret, filled with failure, disgrace, despair, and death. Ultimately, because of Eliza's enduring devotion, it is a story of redemption.

The story of Hamilton's life has the power to transform our lives, as do all stories. Miranda first performed what would become the opening track of *Hamilton* at an official White House dinner. Before he began, he suggested that Hamilton "embodies the word's ability to make a difference." Stories matter. They have the power to fundamentally change the way that we see the world and live our lives. They can inspire us to be the people God created us to be. Before each performance, Chris Jackson led the cast in a prayer circle. He viewed each performance as a deeply spiritual experience. Jackson says, "Theatre has an inherent spirituality to it. To so many people, theatre is their church. It's an opportunity to feel something with other folks. . . . I can't think of many things that facilitate that kind of gathering and communal experience. There's a lot of mention of God, spirits, importance. . . . That's why I don't take it lightly." McCarter describes Jackson's hopes as he leads the cast in prayer, "He closes with the hope that everybody—in the audience, on the stage, and in the orchestra pit—will leave the theatre a better person than they walked in." This, without question, describes my experience. Such is the power of story to transform.

Hamilton the musical is a brilliant work of art. Hamilton the man lived a story steeped in spiritual reality. The combination of these two factors create a powerful thin place that has captured our culture's collective heart and imagination. A thin place that holds the potential of transformation.

* * *

In a keynote address that Miranda gave about the power of theatre, he described two important moments that live theatre offers: moments of transcendence and moments of action. In moments of transcendence, we experience something beyond ourselves and new truths open up in unexpected ways. One begins to see the world through a different lens because of what happens onstage. Moments of action confront us with a truth or decision that demands a response in our lives.

I experienced both of these moments, transcendence and action, countless times throughout *Hamilton*. It explains why this story has so captured our culture's imagination. The show becomes a thin place, a moment of transcendence, that ushers us into God's presence among us. And this thin place experience offers us a moment of action, where we must decide if the story of Alexander Hamilton—a story of grace, forgiveness, death, and redemption—will transform the way we live.

Chapter One

Grace

That Alexander Hamilton became anything at all in this world was a remarkable accomplishment. That he became one of the most influential Founding Fathers of our country seems almost miraculous. To understand the unlikely nature of Hamilton's rise, we need only understand where he came from. In his early years, Hamilton endured more hardship, tragedy, and loss than any person should have to bear in a lifetime.

Hamilton and his older brother James were born into a poor family on the island of Nevis in the West Indies. Their mother Rachel, having fled a previously unhappy marriage without obtaining a divorce, was unable to remarry, and lived in a common-law relationship with the boys' father, James. The circumstances of Rachel's first marriage and her common-law relationship earned her a reputation as a notorious woman, creating a stigma of illegitimacy around James and Alexander.

When Hamilton was a young boy, his father abandoned the family, leaving Rachel to raise the two boys alone. When Hamilton was twelve, Rachel died from a raging fever, a sickness that almost took Hamilton's life as well. Both boys found themselves, at very young ages, orphans in utter poverty.

Their older cousin, a thirty-two-year-old man named Peter Lytton, became the boys' legal guardian. A widower, Peter struggled financially as a result of a number of poor business deals. Only a few months after taking the two boys in, he committed suicide, adding yet another layer of tragedy to Hamilton's life. Chernow sums up the unbelievable loss that Hamilton experienced throughout his early years: "Their father had vanished, their mother had died, their cousin and supposed protector had committed bloody suicide, and their aunt, uncle, and grandmother had all died. James, sixteen, and Alexander, fourteen, were now left alone, largely friendless and penniless. At every step in their rootless, topsy-turvy existence, they had been surrounded by failed, broken, embittered people."

How could this boy, who endured such incredible hardship, end up as an influential Founding Father of our country? Miranda begins his musical with this very question.

The answer begins with yet another devastating tragedy. In 1772, a massive hurricane descended onto St. Croix, causing widespread destruction and loss. Hamilton wrote a letter to describe the horror of the event. Through a series of fortunate circumstances, the letter was published anonymously in a local newspaper. Readers were greatly impressed by the obvious intellect and skill of the author. The young Hamilton interpreted the hurricane as divine retribution from God, and called the people to repentance and faithfulness. Hamilton wrote, "Where now, oh! vile worm, is all thy boasted fortitude and resolution? Death comes rushing on in triumph. . . . See thy wretched helpless state and learn to know thyself. . . . Despise thyself and adore thy God. . . . Succour the miserable and lay up a treasure in heaven."

A few local businessmen felt compelled to act when the seventeen-year-old Hamilton was revealed as the author. Chernow writes, "Hamilton did not know it, but he had just written his way out of poverty. This natural calamity was to prove his salvation. . . . A subscription fund was taken up by local businessmen to send this promising youth to North America to be educated." Hamilton's character sings about this experience, reflecting on how this act of grace changed the entire direction of his life. Everything that Hamilton became, every opportunity afforded to him in America, was made possible by this generous gift. In other words, Hamilton built his life on the foundation of grace.

* * *

What is true of Hamilton is true of all of us. Where would any of us be without the grace of God? Isn't the foundation of each of our lives built squarely on God's grace alone? The story of God's activity in our lives is of course, above all else, a story of grace.

Author Phillip Yancey tells a story about C. S. Lewis attending a religious conference. A debate broke out between experts from around the world, who discussed the unique contribution of Christianity. Lewis walked into the room and asked about their discussion. He answered immediately, "Oh, that's easy. It's grace."

Grace lives at the center of the gospel. Most of us nod in agreement, yet one of the greatest challenges of our lives is actually accepting that grace. Angelica Schuyler, Hamilton's cherished sister-in-law, sings about this struggle in the song "It's Quiet Uptown." She observes that grace is oftentimes too powerful for us to fully understand. We struggle to embrace the reality of grace in our lives. Grace is such a powerful concept that we have a hard time naming it and believing it to be true.

Author David Seamands writes about our struggle to accept God's grace: "Many years ago I was driven to the conclusion that the two major causes of most emotional problems among evangelical Christians are these: the failure to understand, receive, and live out God's unconditional grace and forgiveness; and the failure to give out that unconditional love, forgiveness, and grace to other people. . . . We read, we hear, we believe a good theology of grace. But that's not the way we live. The good news of the gospel of grace has not penetrated the level of our emotions."

We have failed, Seamands suggests, to grasp the central truth of the gospel of Jesus. We fail to understand, receive, and live out God's grace. And every emotional problem we experience connects back to this failure.

This failure manifests itself in my life in a thousand different ways. I struggle mightily with insecurity and shame, oftentimes feeling quite unworthy of God's love. At my worst, I feel intense self-hatred. I have a few relationships broken by unresolved conflict. I struggle to believe that I am actually forgiven by God. All of these emotional challenges I face directly connect with my inability to imagine the possibility of God's grace.

* * *

Hamilton penned a letter to his beloved wife Eliza in the early morning hours before his ill-fated duel with Aaron Burr. He wrote, "This letter, my very dear Eliza, will not be delivered to you unless I shall first have terminated my earthly career to begin, as I humbly hope from redeeming grace and divine mercy, a happy immortality." Hamilton hoped in the idea of God's grace, and recognized his reliance on it alone for the life to come. And yet I can sense the presence of doubt in these words. He hopes that God will grant him grace and mercy, yet a part of him struggles to imagine that possibility. If Hamilton confessed this struggle in what he knew could be his last day on earth, surely that struggle to imagine the possibility of grace manifested itself throughout his life.

Hamilton endured a lifelong struggle with shame, an emotion that tempts us to turn away from the possibility of grace. He encountered failure in his life as well:

Moral failure in his notorious affair with Maria Reynolds.

Political failure and fall from grace, tumbling from the second-highest position in the government to a political exile within a few short years.

Spiritual failure, as he appears to have drifted from his faith during the middle years of his life.

When Hamilton struggled with these failures and the resulting shame, how difficult was it for him to remember in those moments the possibility of grace?

Frank Mason Jr. won the Player of the Year award in college basketball in 2017. An undersized guard, he wasn't highly recruited out of high school. In 2013, The Kansas Jayhawks offered him a scholarship as a back-up plan, and each year in college he continued to improve. His senior year he played at a level beyond what anyone expected. After he won the award, the *Kansas City Star* interviewed his father. He said that he always believed in his son, but that "my imagination wasn't (this) big."

The same is true for most of our lives when it comes to God's grace, and it appears to be true for Hamilton. Our imagination simply isn't big enough.

* * *

A movie called *The Mission* captures this lack of imagination when it comes to God's grace. The movie tells the story of Rodrigo Mendoza, an eighteenth-century slave trader in South America. Rodrigo trapped, kidnapped, and murdered countless native South Americans in his effort to sell them into slavery. He made his living buying and selling human beings.

One day, he returned to the town where the woman he loved lived. She spurned Rodrigo, telling him that she had fallen in love with his brother. The next day, Rodrigo murdered his brother in a fit of rage. Overcome with remorse over the man he had become, he went to a local Jesuit mission and lived there for six months. He spent his days alone in a small cell, hardly eating enough to keep himself alive. He lived in that cell, isolated from everyone, from God, even from himself. Rodrigo felt an overwhelming guilt and shame for the atrocities he had committed.

A Jesuit priest at the mission, Father Gabriel, felt deep compassion for this tortured man. He implored Rodrigo to accept the mercy of God. "There is no mercy for me!" shouted Rodrigo. He could not imagine the possibility of God's grace. His imagination wasn't big enough.

* * *

One of Jesus' most beloved parables is the story of the prodigal son. This parable dares us to expand our imagination when it comes to the mercy, love, and grace of God.

The parable begins with a father and two sons. The younger son asks his father for his share of the estate—a demand that in Jesus' time would have been unheard of as an unimaginable act of disrespect to the father and disloyalty to the family. In essence, the son says to the father, *I wish you were dead.* And yet, the father grants the son's request.

The younger son doesn't want a relationship with the father; he simply wants the father's stuff, specifically his money. The son feels discontent at home, in his life with the father. He wonders if something beyond his current life at home will satisfy him in ways that the father cannot.

Disrespecting a father represented such a serious offense in this culture that the father could have had the son beaten, thrown out of the family, even thrown into prison. The book of Deuteronomy goes so far to say that rebellious sons should be stoned to death. And yet the father knows that he cannot compel the son to stay home and love him. The father knows that the love of the son can only be won through giving him his freedom.

The son takes his inheritance, travels to a distant country, and squanders his wealth in wild living. After he spends every last penny, famine comes. The son takes a job working a farm, feeding another man's pigs. He feels such desperate hunger that he longs to fill his stomach with the slop meant for the pigs.

Jewish law prohibits anyone to eat, or even touch, swine, which were considered unclean animals. That this son ended up at this place, feeding the pigs, would have created a visceral response in Jesus' original audience. The son had hit rock bottom. He had left home, and found himself alone in a distant land where nobody cared about him. He was starving to death with nowhere to turn, surrounded by swine.

* * *

The son ends up at a place we know quite well. This is the place we end up whenever we turn away from the Father, thinking something out there will somehow make us happier, more fulfilled, more satisfied. Author Henri Nouwen writes, "Over and over again I have left home. I have fled the hands of blessing and run off to faraway places searching for love! This is the great tragedy of my life and of the lives of so many I meet on my journey." We have all left home, and every time we do, we participate in the great tragedy of humanity.

Finally, the son comes to his senses. Starving and broke, he realizes his foolishness and devises a plan. He returns home to his father and begs for mercy, "Father, I have sinned against heaven and against you. I am no longer worthy to be called your son; make me like one of your hired servants." The son realizes that even his father's servants enjoy a better life compared to his current reality. At least this plan involves food and shelter.

Even when the son comes to his senses—as he realizes how much better home would be than his current circumstances—he can't even begin to imagine the possibility of grace. The best the son can hope for, in his mind, is the father taking him back as a servant. That the father might offer him grace doesn't even enter into the realm of possibility. His imagination isn't big enough.

In our lives, we experience the same reality. We go off to a distant land, hoping to find something that will satisfy us. We end up isolated, alone, and disappointed. When we come to our senses—finally realizing how empty, meaningless, and unfulfilling this distant land has become—we consider returning home. And yet we pause, wondering if God will welcome us back. We find it almost impossible to imagine grace.

Hamilton appears to have gone through a prodigal son season in his faith during his middle-aged years. In his youth, his letters, poems, and prayers displayed a vibrant and meaningful faith. Toward the end of his life, he returned to that faith with a renewed passion and commitment to God, often spending time praying and reading Scripture with his children. But in the middle years during the Revolution, Chernow notes, "he seemed more skeptical about organized religion," and "refrained from a formal church affiliation despite his wife's steadfast religiosity." It is not difficult to imagine Hamilton in the midst of the horrors of war, struggling to make sense of his faith and the idea of a sovereign God. When Hamilton did decide to return home to the Father, did he struggle with the same thoughts of shame and unworthiness as the prodigal son?

* * *

The prodigal son struggles to imagine the possibility of God's grace because he feels so utterly unworthy. His speech reveals what he believes: "I have sinned against heaven and you. I am no longer worthy to be called your son."

The first half of his speech is true. The son did indeed sin against his father, disrespecting and embarrassing him in front of the entire community. The son rejected the father for the sake of his money, then used the father's money to satisfy his own selfish and debased desires.

But the second half of the son's speech is not true. Like the son, we often make a subtle shift from truth to untruth, believing and telling ourselves statements that simply are not true. "I am not longer worthy to be called your son," the son tells himself.

The son believes that his worthiness is based on his behavior, his decisions, his failures. And because of his mistakes, he is no longer worthy to be called a son.

This belief brings up a critical question for our lives: What is our worthiness based on? We make the same mistake as the son, thinking our worthiness depends on ourselves, our behavior, our actions. When we succeed in life, when things go well, when we obey God and resist temptation, we feel worthy of his love. We feel worthy to be called his son or daughter.

But when we fail—when our brokenness overwhelms us, when we give into temptation, when we end up in a distant land feeding the pigs—we repeat the lie of the prodigal son, "I am not worthy to be called God's son." We believe our worthiness depends on our performance, which undercuts the truth of God's grace. "If by grace," Paul writes in the book of Romans, "then it cannot be based on works; if it were, grace would no longer be grace."

What if our worthiness did not depend on us? What if our fundamental worthiness as human beings came from outside of ourselves, based on God's grace, and God's grace alone?

Author Phillip Yancey defines grace this way: "Grace means there is nothing we can do to make God love us more. . . . And grace means there is nothing we can do to make God love us less. . . . Grace means that God already loves us as much as an infinite God can possibly love."

Grace means that our worthiness has nothing to do with our performance. If it did, grace wouldn't be grace. If Yancey is right, our performance has zero impact on the way God feels about us, on the way God loves us. To quote Yancey again, "Grace teaches us that God loves us because of who God is, not because of who we are. Categories of worthiness do not apply." We are worthy because we are made in the image of God, because he calls us his children, because he loves us—not because of anything we have or have not done to deserve that love.

Hamilton experienced so much success in his life that he surely struggled with finding his worth in his performance and accomplishments, rather than in God's love and grace. He achieved a level of success that he never could have imagined, rising from an orphan born in poverty to second in command of the new US Government. And yet success can be a double-edged sword—it seduces us into thinking our worth depends on it. I wonder how much of Hamilton's relentless drive was an attempt to somehow earn the gift of grace that brought him to America? To prove to himself and to the world that he was worthy of that grace? Yet any attempt to earn grace contradicts its very nature. Grace cannot be based on works; if it were, grace would no longer be grace.

* * *

The prodigal son returns home to the father, filled with anxiety and fear on the long walk home. He knows he deeply wronged and shamed his father. He questions and doubts how his father will respond. Will he accept him, even as a lowly servant?

The son never could have imagined the father's response: "But while he was still a long way off, his father saw him and was filled with compassion for him; he ran to his son, threw his arms around him and kissed him." Jesus offers here a picture of the father, looking out to the horizon, longing for his son to return home. How many days had the father spent, hoping beyond hope, that today would be the day that the beloved son would return?

The father's first response is not anger, judgment, hatred, or rejection. His first response is compassion, for the road his son had been on, for mistakes made, and for the suffering they it caused. Compassion for the shame he knew his son felt, for the feelings of unworthiness he carried home with him.

When the father saw his beloved son, he ran to meet him—an act no respected elder would perform in Jewish culture. It was considered a shameful act to run in public. When the father runs, he takes the shame of the son upon himself. The community of people shamefully judged the son as he walked home. Now they shift their judgment toward the father for such a shameful response. New Testament scholar Richard Vinson suggests that in this act, the shame has been transferred from the son to the father.

The father runs, embraces his son, and begins to kiss him. The son goes into his speech that he rehearsed a thousand times. "I have sinned, I am no longer worthy to be called your son." Even in the moment that the son receives grace from his father, he still can't imagine it as a possibility. The father actively offers grace, but the son can't see it. All he can see is his own unworthiness.

But the father isn't listening. He calls out to his servants, "Bring the best robe and put it on my son! Put a ring on his finger! Find sandals for his feet! Slaughter the fattened calf for a celebration! This son of mine was dead and is alive again; he was lost and is found!"

The father reminds his son of his true identity, an identity that had been buried and forgotten underneath layers of mistakes and failures. The father declares that he will make the determination of his son's worthiness. The father's love and grace overwhelm the son's brokenness and failure. The apostle Paul writes, "But sin didn't, and doesn't have a chance in competition with the aggressive forgiveness we call *grace*. When it's sin versus grace, grace wins hands down."

* * *

The question for our lives is simple: Can we believe in the possibility of God's grace? Can we begin to understand it, receive it, and live it out? Can we stretch our imagination so that it becomes big enough to believe in the truth of God's grace, even for us?

To experience God's grace, we must follow the example of the prodigal son, who comes to his senses and returns home. The Bible calls this act repentance, a word that means, literally, to turn around.

Repenting involves looking at our lives and recognizing our failures, our faults, our brokenness. It means coming to terms with all the ways we have left home and rejected God. And then we repent; we return home, confident that God will offer us grace.

* * *

For six months, Rodrigo Mendoza sat in a cell at the Jesuit Mission, utterly defeated by the sins of his life. Father Gabriel entered into his cell one day, frustrated with Mendoza's inability to receive forgiveness and move forward with his life. He talked to Mendoza about redemption. "There is no redemption for me," Mendoza angrily responded. He could not imagine the possibility of God's grace.

Father Gabriel asked him if he had the courage to choose his penance. Mendoza again replied, "There is no penance hard enough for me."

"But do you dare try it?" Gabriel asked.

"Do I dare? Do you dare see it fail?" responded Mendoza.

Gabriel imagined a penance that would push Mendoza to his limits. They planned a climb to the top of the mountain, the home of the tribal people Mendoza enslaved. During the climb, Mendoza bound himself to a net filled with armor and weapons. Mendoza struggled to make progress on this treacherous climb carrying this heavy burden.

They finally reached the top, and the tribal people came out to meet them at the edge of their village. When they recognized Mendoza, chaos ensued. The whole tribe yelled and tried to determine what to do. One man ran up to Mendoza and placed a blade at his throat. This was the death Mendoza deserved, the death he might have even been longing for.

But then, instead of slitting Mendoza's throat, the man cut the rope that bound him to the netting and hurled it over a cliff. Mendoza had been freed from his burden—freed by the very people he had murdered, kidnapped, and enslaved.

Mendoza wept. And then, his weeping turned into laughter. For the first time in the film, Mendoza smiled. Joy exploded across his face as he experienced grace. His imagination had been expanded. His future opened up to all kinds of new possibilities. Such is the power of grace.

* * *

The grace that formed the foundation of Hamilton's life is now being offered to students throughout New York City. Through a partnership with the Theatre Development Fund (TDF), six hundred students were given the opportunity to attend a matinee performance of *Hamilton*. Ginger Bartkoski Meageher of TDF said that the experience moved the students deeply. Any time we encounter grace, it transforms us.

The Rockefeller Foundation expanded this grace significantly. A $1.5 million gift enabled twenty thousand students from New York public schools to see *Hamilton* in 2016. *Hamilton* producers hope to offer a similar program to other cities on the national tour. These tickets represent grace given to these students, as many of them never could have obtained them on their own. This gift of grace could possibly transform their lives, and transform the givers' lives in the process. After one of the student performances, Miranda tweeted, "The student matinees are, it turns out, the highlights of my life. I can't begin to describe how it feels."

* * *

This grace, the grace God longs to give us, is possible for each and every one of us. Our souls long for this grace; in truth, we live by it. Grace remains present to us, each and every moment of our lives.

In the novel *The Diary of a Country Priest*, a young priest struggles with insecurity, doubt, fear, and faith as he ministers to the people in his small parish. He struggles to imagine and experience the possibility of grace. He believes himself unworthy. As the story ends, he finally comes to peace with himself and with God. His very last journal entry reads, "Grace is everywhere."

God's grace is everywhere. Our world overflows with it. We just have to learn to imagine the possibility of it. Yancey says we must learn to see "through grace-tinted lenses."

When that happens, we begin to see grace everywhere that we look. We begin to imagine it as a possibility, even for us. We begin to understand, receive, and live out God's grace. In doing so, that grace leads us into all kinds of possibilities for our lives.

Chapter Two

Shame

The shame Hamilton experienced as a child hounded him throughout his life. Born into the stigma of illegitimacy, Hamilton grew quite familiar to the stinging taunt of "bastard," a painful label in the eighteenth century. Hamilton, Chernow writes, lived with "wretched feelings of shame and degradation," was a "mass of insecurities that he usually kept well hidden," and constantly lived with "the wounds left by his accursed boyhood." No matter how far he traveled and how much success he found, he remained "the hypersensitive boy from the West Indies." Hamilton himself wrote, "my birth is the subject of the most humiliating criticism."

John Adams, a political enemy of Hamilton in the early years of the republic, vocalized the shame Hamilton felt internally, calling him "the bastard brat of a Scotch peddler" and a "Creole bastard." Adams also simply referred to Hamilton as "the foreigner." New York Governor George Clinton attacked Hamilton's illegitimacy in published essays under the pen name "Cato." These insults give insight into the constant ignominy that Hamilton suffered, which in turn fueled a deep-seated sense of shame.

* * *

Hamilton met Eliza Schuyler in 1777, while in Albany for a meeting with General Horatio Gates. Their love blossomed during the winter of 1780, while she stayed with relatives in Morristown, New Jersey, at the same time the Continental Army camped there. Hamilton began courting her and they spent almost every evening together. One of Hamilton's friends noticed the romance and suggested that "Hamilton is a gone man." After a month of courtship, they decided to marry.

During the infancy of their relationship, Hamilton felt ashamed of his illegitimacy and humble origins and unworthy to marry into Eliza's wealthy and prominent family. We see this shame in Miranda's musical when Hamilton first meets Eliza's older sister, Angelica. In a culture obsessed with family status, Angelica asks about his family origins. Hamilton responds by deflecting the question and focuses instead on his future and what he plans to accomplish with his life.

Chernow surmises that during Hamilton and Eliza's courtship, Hamilton confessed his illegitimacy to Eliza's father, General Schuyler, who responded graciously, "I am pleased with every instance of delicacy in those who are dear to me, and I think I read your soul on that occasion you mention." Sharing shameful secrets with his future father-in-law could not have been easy for Hamilton.

Letters Hamilton wrote to Eliza during this courtship expressed his insecurities. "I know I have talents and a good heart, but why am I not handsome? Why have I not every acquirement that can embellish human nature? Why have I not fortune. . . ?"

Elsewhere, he voiced insecurities about his lack of wealth, questioning whether he deserved Eliza as his bride. "I have not concealed my circumstances from my Betsey [his nickname for her]; they are far from splendid. . . . I cannot however forbear entreating you to realize our union on the dark side and satisfy, without deceiving yourself, how far your affection for me can make you happy in a privation of those elegancies to which you have been accustomed. . . . examine well your heart." We can only assume that Eliza did examine her heart, and found it overflowing with love for this bright, young, immigrant orphan. Nonetheless, the shame that surfaced during Hamilton's courtship of Eliza haunted, influenced, and motivated him until the day that he died.

* * *

Imagining Hamilton's shame isn't difficult for most of us. We all struggle with shame, the feeling that we are not good enough. Similar to guilt, another familiar emotion, shame has one slight but crucial difference. Guilt focuses on our behavior; we feel bad for what we do. Shame, however, focuses on our very selves. When we feel shame, we feel bad for who we *are*.

In a TED talk, research professor and author Brene Brown explains that guilt says, "I'm sorry, I made a mistake." Shame says, "I'm sorry, I am a mistake." Author Lewis Smedes writes, "The feeling of shame is about our very selves. . . . It tells us that we *are* unworthy. Totally. . . . And to feel that is a life-wearing heaviness."

Like Hamilton, my shame too often haunts, influences, and motivates my life. I am familiar with that life-wearing heaviness.

Any time I fall short of being the person I want to be, when I lose patience with my kids, tell an untruth, or judge another, shame attacks. I feel unworthy, my sense of value being ripped away. I am convinced that I am not accepted or loved, that I am not enough. At times the shame so overwhelms me that I begin to hate myself and who I have become. Such is the heaviness and burden of shame.

And yet, shame can at times represent a healthy response to what we have done. Smedes writes, "A creature meant to be a little less than God is likely to feel a deep dissatisfaction with herself if she falls a notch below the splendid human being she is meant to be. If we never feel shame, we may have lost contact with the person we most truly are."

God made us in his image and calls us to live out that identity. God created us to love, to live holy lives, to serve others, to put others above ourselves. When we fail to live out that calling, healthy shame reminds us of our deepest calling, our truest identity. When we live selfishly, fail to love, are filled with pride, or give into lust, shame points us back from our flawed nature to who God created us to be. Smedes writes, "Shame, we are told, is the painful feeling of being a flawed human being. Well, what if, in fact, we *are* flawed human beings? All of us. Cracked vessels. Wheels out of alignment. The heart of us slightly off center. What if none of us is quite a match for the self we could be?"

* * *

The prophet Jeremiah implores his listeners to exhibit a healthy shame. In the years leading up to the Babylonian exile, he preaches to the people of Judea who have collectively turned away from God, who live unfaithfully, who forgot who God called them to be—and he preaches to all of us now, all these millennia later. Jeremiah's harshest criticism? The people lost their capacity for shame. "Are they ashamed of their detestable conduct? No, they have no shame at all; they do not even know how to blush." When we lose this capacity for shame, we are in danger of losing touch with who God created us to be.

In Paul's first letter to the Corinthians, he writes to another group of people who have turned away from God, who live unfaithfully, who forget who they were called to be. Paul confronts the believers in Corinth about their disobedience and writes "I say this to shame you." Paul longs for them to feel a healthy shame.

* * *

Far more common than healthy shame, sadly, is our experience of unhealthy shame. This shame tells us that we are fundamentally flawed and broken. That we are not enough, that somehow our failures render us unworthy of love and acceptance.

Smedes tells the story of a gifted piano player named Lech Koplinski, who lived in the city of Karpov. Because he had no connections with the concert world, Koplinski played the piano at a local cabaret. His friend, Chenska Wolenka, an attractive woman who frequented the cabaret, longed to see Lech find success as a concert pianist. One night, when a concert producer came to the cabaret, Chenska befriended him, hoping to connect him with Lech.

Smedes writes, "The producer of concerts made Chenska a proposition. If she would make love with him, he would see to it that Lech got his chance on the concert stage. She agreed, and in his bed made good on her bargain. The producer made good on his as well. Lech did indeed play the piano on the concert stage. Lech went off on concert tours, became a star, and did not come back to the cabaret. All that Chenska had left over was a deep shame of herself. One early morning in May she jumped from her apartment window to her death in a Karpov alley. Taped to her mirror was this sentence: *I am filth*."

"I did, therefore I am; this is the fatal equation," writes Smedes.

Chenska could not distinguish between what she had done and who she was, the two inextricably wound together. Because she had done something she perceived as so despicable, she considered herself filth. She felt unworthy of love and acceptance. Unworthy, even, of life itself.

Perhaps Hamilton felt this unworthiness when he wrote to his good friend, John Laurens, "I am disgusted with everything in this world but yourself and a *very* few more honest fellows and I have no other wish than as soon as possible to make a brilliant exit. 'Tis a weakness, but I feel I am not fit for this terrestrial country." Hamilton thought often about death and martyrdom, as Miranda's musical captures when Hamilton sings about how often he imagines death. Perhaps Hamilton's shame and feelings of unworthiness manifested themselves in this preoccupation with death, this feeling of "not being fit for this terrestrial country."

* * *

These examples warn us of the unbearable pain triggered by unhealthy shame. We see through Hamilton how the belief of being unworthy of love, of acceptance, even at times, of life itself can shadow us in a thousand different ways, haunting and influencing our every move. In the gospel, however, we find freedom from this damning shame.

In Mark's gospel, Jesus encounters a man who, like Hamilton, lives with a deep sense of shame. The source of this man's shame came not from an illegitimate birth, but rather from a debilitating skin disease called leprosy. Lepers, in biblical times, suffered a relentless barrage of shame. Considered an extremely contagious disease, lepers lived outside the city, isolated from home and family.

The shame of this disease continues today. In India, people found with the disease are still sent to live in colonies outside of major cities. A *US News & World Report* article told the story of Yadav, a man diagnosed with leprosy in his thirties. He immediately lost his job, and his parents asked him to leave home—concerned that his disease would harm his sister's marital prospects.

In biblical times, the physical aspects of the disease only partially motivated separation; a spiritual component also existed. New Testament scholar David Neale writes of the spiritual component in banishment: "Leprosy in Jesus' day was a disease with complex social and religious implications, which blurred the line between physical sickness and sin." People interpreted leprosy both as a physical ailment and a spiritual consequence of sin and disobedience, which led to Jewish laws forcing separation of "unclean" lepers from the temple or synagogue. If a leper ever entered a city, the law required the leper to shout out to passersby, "Unclean! Unclean!"

In this way, the Jewish community branded lepers as fundamentally flawed human beings. Unworthy. Unaccepted. Unloved. Because of the belief that their own sin and disobedience to God caused this disease, lepers experienced isolation and unimaginable loneliness.

The closest modern-day comparison I can make is to the homosexual community. In the 1980s and 1990s, more Americans came out of the closet than ever before to tell friends and family they were gay. Many of these men and women experienced gut wrenching shame, isolation, and rejection. Philip Yancey tells a story of a man who had been rejected by his family for more than ten years when, finally, he was invited home to celebrate Thanksgiving. Yancey writes, "His mother seated him apart from the family, at a separate table set with Chinette plates and plastic utensils." This man's banishment captures the intensity of shame a leper in biblical times felt.

* * *

In Luke's gospel narrative, Jesus enters a town when a leper approaches him and falls at his feet, his face to the ground. He begs Jesus, "Lord, if you are willing, you can make me clean."

This man had been told his entire life: You are unworthy, unacceptable, unloved. He must have oftentimes believed this as the deepest truth about himself, living with a daily sense of overwhelming shame. Yet in this story, this leper dares to believe a different narrative about himself, and about Jesus. He dares to believe that he is more than his disease and imperfections, and that Jesus can somehow free him from the shame that had so completely obliterated his life.

I once heard a story about a man who, living alone, went to the barber once a week, just to experience the touch of another person. I imagine the leper, like this man, longing for the sensation of human touch, forbidden in the leper's case by the law.

In response, Jesus offers a remarkable grace. He reaches out his hand, and touches the leper. I love to imagine the emotion that must have poured out of the man with leprosy in that moment. "There are few gestures as profound, loving, and healing as human touch," writes David Lose, the president of Lutheran Theological Seminary. In touching the man with leprosy, Jesus offers him a beautiful gift. In that touch, Jesus affirms to him, "You are worthy. You are loved. You are enough."

Jesus then says to the man, "I am willing, be clean," and the leprosy immediately leaves his body. Jesus touched the leper, but—despite the law—Jesus is not made unclean. And Jesus takes the reversal one step further, his integrity and wholeness overcoming and healing the leper's brokenness.

* * *

The love and acceptance Eliza offered to a young, insecure Hamilton reflects the gift Jesus bestowed upon the leper. Eliza's love communicated to Alexander, "You are worthy. You are accepted. You are enough." Her love transformed him, and in her presence, his shame slowly melted away. Hamilton himself wrote about how much the love Eliza offered him transformed his life, "I was once determined to let my existence and American liberty end together. My Betsey has given me a motive to outlive my pride."

* * *

Too often we feel like the leper in the gospel story. We look at our lives and see brokenness, failures, and imperfections. We feel overwhelmed by unhealthy shame and isolate ourselves, not wanting to infect anyone else with our brokenness. "Unclean!" we cry out, not with words, but with our actions, our body language, our eyes. We begin to believe the lies that whisper to us that, because we make mistakes, we are a mistake. We believe that we are unworthy, unloved, unaccepted.

Will we find the courage to follow the leper's example, to bring our shame to the feet of Jesus? What if we fell at Jesus' feet, confessing our brokenness to him, begging him to forgive us and make us whole again?

If we take this risk, Jesus will reach out his hand to touch us, offering love and accepting us as we are and not as we should be. Our brokenness doesn't infect or repulse him. Rather, his holiness, integrity, and love transform us. In that great reversal, we find freedom from our shame. The apostle Paul wrote to the church in Corinth, "God made him who had no sin to be sin for us, so that in him we might become the righteousness of God." Jesus took our shame upon the cross, and now through his healing touch, we take on Jesus' righteousness, holiness, and wholeness.

* * *

Confessing our shame to a safe person—a risk Hamilton took in his early letters to Eliza—moves us toward bringing our shame to Jesus. Sharing our brokenness with another requires vulnerability and risking the possibility of rejection. But it also opens up the possibility of acceptance, love, and grace. The possibility that someone might remind us, "You are enough." When someone else offers us that gift, we find healing from our shame. The author of the book of James says, "Confess your sins to each another . . . so that we may be healed." Dietrich Bonhoeffer describes the grim alternative: "He who is alone with his sin is utterly alone."

"Empathy," says Brene Brown in her TED talk, "is the antidote to shame. Put shame in a petri dish, and it needs three things to grow: secrecy, silence, judgment. Without these three realities, shame cannot survive." When we follow the example of the leper, we refuse to live in secrecy and silence. When someone else responds to our brokenness with empathy and love, rather than judgment, shame melts away.

* * *

A good friend of mine once shared his brokenness and shame with me. He confessed that he was an alcoholic, that his drinking had spiraled out of control. One night after drinking too much, he drove home drunk, crashed his car, and spent the night in jail. He realized at that moment that he needed help. He confessed his drinking to his wife, joined Alcoholics Anonymous, and began walking the courageous path toward sobriety.

My friend felt great trepidation when he shared his story with me, fearful of my response, of whether or not I would accept him. He displayed incredible courage in confessing his shame.

When he finished his confession, I told him that I loved him. That we all have demons we battle. That knowing about his alcoholism didn't change the way I felt about him. I thanked him for sharing his vulnerabilities. His brokenness didn't repel me or make me think less of him; it actually caused me to love him more.

I also told him that I hoped my response reflected to him the unconditional love and grace of God—that my response might somehow point him to the truth that God's love overwhelms all our shame. If I responded to his brokenness with acceptance and compassion, how much more does God respond to us in this manner?

If my friend hadn't said anything to anyone, if he had kept his shame a secret, he would have created an environment for shame to thrive. He would have cut himself off from the possibility of forgiveness, grace, and acceptance, from God or anyone else. He exposed his shame, and in doing so, experienced the unconditional love that annihilates shame.

* * *

In *Hamilton*, Eliza and Alexander share an intimate moment during the Revolutionary War, a moment captured in the song "That Would Be Enough." In the musical, Washington has sent Hamilton home from the front lines, at Eliza's request, because of her pregnancy. Hamilton struggles with leaving the front lines, where he has an opportunity to improve his fortunes in life. During the song, Hamilton reveals his battles with inadequacy, his feeling that he is not enough. He asks her if she will be content married to a poor man.

Eliza reaches out and touches her husband, offering love and acceptance. Over and over, she sings to him that he is all that she wants. In the midst of Hamilton's shame and feelings of inadequacy, she reminds him that he is enough. She counteracts the voice of shame inside of Alexander's head, just as God longs to do for each of us.

Chapter Three

Faith

Hamilton practiced a sincere and authentic faith throughout much of his life. His faith blossomed as a young boy in the Caribbean, exhibited by his eloquent and spiritual writing in response to the hurricane that devastated the island of St. Croix. The young Hamilton interpreted the events of his life through a spiritual lens. He composed another hymn in his youth, which articulates an intimate knowledge of life with God. Entitled "The Soul Ascending into Bliss," he wrote, "Hark! Hark! A voice from yonder sky / Methinks I hear my Saviour cry / Come, gentle spirit, come away / Come to the Lord without delay. . . . O Lamb of God! thrice gracious Lord / Now, now I feel how true thy word / Translated to this happy place / This blessed vision of thy face." Eliza preserved a copy of this poem. It reminded her of Hamilton's faith in God.

When Hamilton arrived in New York City, two of his earliest acquaintances were clergymen, Dr. John Rodgers and the Reverend John M. Mason. While at King's College, Hamilton participated in the school's rhythms of religious devotion, involving daily morning chapel, evening prayers, and church services twice on Sunday. One school friend, Robert Troup, observed that Hamilton "was attentive to public worship and in the habit of praying on his knees night and morning. . . . I have often been powerfully affected by the fervor and eloquence of his prayers."

Despite his religious commitment in his earlier years, during middle-age Hamilton drifted from his religious devotion. Chernow writes, "Like the other founders and thinkers of the Enlightenment, he was disturbed by religious fanaticism and tended to associate organized religion with superstition." While serving as treasury secretary, he said, "The world has been scourged with many fanatical sects in religion who, inflamed by a sincere but mistaken zeal, have perpetuated under the idea of serving God the most atrocious crimes."

In his later years, he returned to the faith of his youth with fervor. Chernow writes, "It is striking how religion preoccupied Hamilton during his final years." His son, John Church Hamilton, recounted how his father "experienced a resurgence of his youthful fervor, prayed daily, and scribbled many notes in the margin of the family Bible." Hamilton hoped to one day build a chapel for his children on land he purchased north of the city.

The final letter he wrote to his beloved wife Eliza before his duel with Aaron Burr was steeped in religious language. He wrote about God's grace and life after death. He also encouraged Eliza, in the event of his death, to find support and comfort in God.

Hamilton experienced alternating seasons of authentic faith and genuine doubt. In other words, Hamilton's spiritual life reflects the experience of every human being who attempts to walk closely with God. I can't imagine my faith in God without the consistent reality of doubt. Author Frederick Buechner writes, "Without somehow destroying me in the process, how could God reveal himself in a way that would leave no room for doubt? If there were no room for doubt, there would be no room for me."

* * *

Can you remember the moments of your life that created strong faith? Moments when God's presence felt tangible and real, when God answered your prayers in powerful ways? The moments when you believed, *really believed*, in God and his love for you?

In college, I built a friendship with a girl named Allison. We spent a significant amount of time together and I quickly fell for her, but lacked the courage to ask her on an official date. During my cowardly inaction, another boy asked her out, and she started dating him. Heartbroken and devastated, I prayed that God would open a door for me, or perhaps hit this boy with a bus. I prayed that I would end up with Allison.

That winter, Allison and I went on a college ski trip. We stayed up late one night talking, and I found the courage to tell her that I loved her. Thankfully, she felt the same way, asked me what took so long, and we started dating. Allison's response that night filled me with faith. God proved himself present and powerful and answered my prayers.

Can you recall the moments of your life that uncovered strong doubts? The moments when God felt absent, when he didn't answer your prayers, when you experienced tragedy, heartache, and disappointment?

In his book *Faith & Doubt*, John Ortberg shares a story that created doubt in his life. His friends had a beautiful baby daughter. One summer day, the mother took her playpen into the backyard, where they owned a pool. Ortberg writes,

> The phone rang, and her daughter was in the playpen, so she went in to answer the phone. Her daughter tugged on the wall of that playpen, and the hinge that held the side up gave way. It didn't have to. God could have stopped it. God could have reached down from heaven and straightened it out and kept that playpen up. He didn't. The hinge gave way, and the side came down, and the baby crawled out, and heaven was silent. When that mom came outside, she saw the beautiful little body of her beloved daughter at the bottom of that pool. It was the beginning of a pain that no words could name.

We all experience tragedy and loss in this life, and the natural response is doubt. How could this happen? Where was God? Why didn't he save me from this suffering and pain?

In our spiritual lives, we often understand faith and doubt as opposing categories. We either have faith or doubt, the two don't crossover. Life with God proves much subtler than that. Author Michael Novak writes, "Doubt is not so much a dividing line that separates people into different camps as it is a razor's edge that runs through every soul."

* * *

In the Gospel of Mark, after his transfiguration, Jesus climbs down a mountain with his three closest disciples. While on the mountain, Jesus' face began to shine like the sun, his clothes became whiter than anyone could bleach them, and he shared a conversation with Elijah and Moses. Afterward, Jesus and the three disciples descend the mountain and notice the other disciples surrounded by an angry, argumentative crowd. When the crowd sees Jesus, they rush over to him.

A father explains that he brought his son, possessed by a spirit that rendered the boy mute. This spirit also threw the boy to the ground, caused the boy to become rigid and foam at the mouth, and even threw the boy into fire or water to try to kill him.

Imagine the trauma this father experienced. A parent experiences no greater pain than watching their child suffer. This child had suffered greatly, causing the father real doubt. Why does my son suffer? Why won't you help him, God? The father had likely spent years praying, begging God to heal his son, but heaven remained silent.

Then, the father hears about Jesus, who performs miracles, heals people, and casts out demons. A spark of faith develops. He dares to believe that Jesus might heal his son, and in a tangible act of faith, the father brings his son to Jesus.

When he arrives, Jesus is up on the mountain praying, but his disciples promise to help. Earlier in Mark, Jesus gave the disciples authority to drive out demons, which they had successfully done a number of times. They assume they could repeat their past accomplishments.

The father's doubt recedes and his faith grows. When the disciples declare they can heal him, he surges with hope. Finally, his son will be healed from suffering. The disciples attempt to cast out the demon, but nothing happens. They look around at each other with confused looks on their faces. The father's doubt rushes back, stronger than before. His hopes crushed by the disciples' failure.

When Jesus arrives, the father shares his desperation with him, "If you can do anything, take pity on us and help us." Understandably, the father has doubts about Jesus' ability to heal his son. His prayers have gone unanswered, and the disciples had just failed to drive out this spirit. If this man had seen Jesus up on the mountain, with his true identity revealed, he wouldn't have expressed doubt. Many times, our doubt stems from our inability to understand Jesus' true identity and power.

"'If you can'?" replies Jesus, "Everything is possible for one who believes."

And then this father utters a prayer familiar to every one of us: "I do believe, help me overcome my unbelief!"

This father articulates a profound truth of the spiritual life: the coexistence of faith and doubt. Both live in our hearts, as they did in Hamilton's, intersecting and overlapping from moment to moment.

* * *

One of the most common manifestations of doubt attacks us in the form of self-doubt. The disciples surely struggled with self-doubt after they failed to cast out the spirit from the boy.

After their failure, they must have questioned themselves and felt embarrassment and shame. "What did we do wrong? Why were we unable to cast out this spirit?" They probably even questioned their worth and value as disciples of Jesus. "Maybe I'm not good enough. Maybe my best days are behind me. Maybe I'm destined to be a failure."

I have consistently struggled with self-doubt throughout my life and ministry career. As a pastor for almost twenty years, so many ministry circumstances have not met my expectations. Low attendance at services, canceled events due to lack of interest, or families leaving our church community create discouragement that quickly morphs into self-doubt. I can go to a very dark place at a stunning pace. "I'm not very good at this," I tell myself. "I'm not a talented enough leader or communicator. I probably should do something different with my life. Time to update the resume."

Blogger Karen Salmansohn encourages us in this battle against self-doubt: "Ban, delete, shred, obliterate the words: 'I'm not good enough.'" I believe her words and want to live by them, but I struggle to accept them when self-doubt attacks.

Hamilton struggled with this self-doubt throughout his life as well. Miranda writes this struggle into Hamilton's character: "This swagger, built on a bedrock of total insecurity, is the contradiction that is our Hamilton." Swagger and insecurity, faith and doubt, is the contradiction that describes all of our lives.

* * *

The first step in our battle with doubt is simply acknowledging our struggle. The father models this in his prayer to Jesus:

"Help me overcome my unbelief!" Too often we perceive doubt as weakness or failure, which causes embarrassment, shame, or guilt. We find freedom by acknowledging the presence of doubt in our spiritual journey.

The first step in the Alcoholics Anonymous twelve-step program of personal recovery encourages addicts to admit they are powerless over alcohol, and that life has become unmanageable. Until we acknowledge any struggle in our lives, growth eludes us. You cannot change what you do not acknowledge, a counselor once told me.

Sharing your doubts with a trustworthy friend offers a tangible step toward acknowledgement. When we share our doubts with others, we get them out of our heads and find encouragement and solidarity with others who can empathize with our struggle. Paul writes to the church in Galatia, "Carry each other's burdens, and in this way you will fulfill the law of Christ." How can we carry each other's burdens and doubts if we do not share them with one another?

I remember a season when I found myself in a dark place, struggling with discouragement and doubting my calling. The church I led at the time felt stagnant, and I began to imagine its slow demise into oblivion. During one of my lowest weeks, I had a haircut appointment with a woman who had cut my hair for more than ten years. She asked me how I was doing. Five years earlier, I would have lied, pretended everything was fine, and simply made small talk. I wouldn't have risked being vulnerable and sharing my doubts.

But on this day, I took a risk. "Honestly, I'm not doing very well," I shared with her. I explained the discouragement I felt, and how it had led me to a place of despair and doubt.

Over the next thirty minutes, she shared incredible insights into my life, into patterns of behavior she had seen play out in our conversations over the years. She brought clarity, truth, and encouragement to me that day. As I left, I recaptured a sense of faith that overcame my oppressive doubts. I acknowledged my doubt to someone else, and it helped move me toward faith. A few days later this woman, who doesn't identify herself as a Christian, texted me this: "It came to me yesterday. . . . Kevin, you spread his word and let God build HIS church. That's on him, not you! Hope that doesn't sound crazy, but those are the words I heard loud and clear (repetitively) as I was thinking and sending you positive thoughts. Hang in there."

Hamilton confessed his doubts and insecurities primarily to his wife Eliza and his good friend John Laurens. Chernow writes, "However loaded with superabundant talent, Hamilton was a mass of insecurities that he usually kept well hidden. He always had to fight the residual sadness of the driven man, the unspoken melancholy of the prodigy, the wounds left by his accursed boyhood. Only to John Laurens and Eliza Schuyler did he confide his fears." Chernow describes a letter written to Laurens "that showed him steeped in inconsolable gloom. . . . [written in] a despairing tone that was to crop up throughout his life."

* * *

After we acknowledge our doubts, taking a tangible step toward faith becomes our next move. The father models this by bringing his son to Jesus. He wasn't certain that Jesus could heal his son; doubt still lurked inside of him. But he moved forward in faith despite those doubts—a step that served as the catalyst that healed his son.

The book of James encourages us to see faith as action and movement. "What good is it, my brothers and sisters, if someone claims to have faith but has no deeds? Can such faith save them? Suppose a brother or sister is without clothes and daily food. If one of you says to them, 'Go in peace; keep warm and well fed,' but does nothing about their physical needs, what good is it? In the same way, faith by itself, if it is not accompanied by action, is dead." The context of this passage is a call to serve the poor, but the universal truth stands: faith requires action, or else it is not faith.

* * *

In May of 1776, Washington and his Continental Army prepared to defend New York against the coming British invasion, a force Washington knew to be vastly superior to his. The British would hold significant advantages in both the number and quality of soldiers, their weaponry, and military experience. Washington must have raged with doubts at the battle that loomed before him. Miranda captures the dark reality in Washington's mind in the song, "Right Hand Man." Washington acknowledges his doubts and shares them with the audience, drawing them into the angst that he feels.

And yet, in the face of crushing doubt, Washington moves toward faith. In May of 1776, the Continental Congress declared a day "to be observed as a day of fasting, humiliation, and prayer, humbly to supplicate the mercy of almighty God, that it would please Him to pardon all our manifold sins and transgressions, and to prosper the arms of the united colonies, and finally establish the peace and freedom of America upon a solid and lasting foundation." Washington immediately commanded "all officers, and soldiers, to pay strict obedience to the Orders of the Continental Congress."

Washington encouraged his men to move toward faith, to fast, humble themselves, and pray. He dared to believe, despite the enormous odds facing him, that they might emerge victorious, that God might act on their behalf. His faith became action and movement, as it would over and over again throughout this horrible conflict. Without Washington's habit of moving toward faith in the face of doubt, the American Revolution would have been lost before it had ever begun.

* * *

We see this characteristic in so many heroes of the faith. Mother Teresa traveled to Calcutta in 1948, following a call she received from the Lord to serve the poorest of the poor. For almost fifty years, she faithfully served the poor, offering love, compassion, and sacrifice rarely seen in our world. And yet throughout the second half of her life, she felt the absence of God and struggled deeply with doubt. She wrote to her spiritual director, "Jesus has a very special love for you. As for me, the silence and the emptiness is so great that I look and do not see, listen and do not hear." She described this absence as a "dryness, darkness, loneliness, and torture." She compared her experience to hell, and said it drove her to doubt the existence of heaven and even of God. Despite experiencing these crushing doubts for decades, she never abandoned her faith or her work. She pressed on, moving toward faith in the midst of her doubts.

* * *

One of my favorite historical details from Hamilton and Burr's duel involves plans Hamilton made for later that day. Hamilton must have struggled with doubts as he met Burr on the dueling ground. Would he survive? Would Burr aim with the intent to kill? Would he ever see his family again? Or would he escape unscathed? In the face of these doubts, Hamilton set an appointment with a client to work on a legal matter later that morning. Hamilton moved forward in faith that he would survive and attend his meeting following his duel with Burr. He models for us faith in the face of doubt—although in this instance, his faith proved tragically misplaced in the hands of Aaron Burr. Yet this disastrous outcome doesn't negate the underlying spiritual principle: When facing doubts, God calls us to move forward in faith. As we do so, we must remember that the outcome is oftentimes beyond our ability to control.

Chapter Four

Initiative

The trajectory of Hamilton's life could most accurately be explained by one ever-present characteristic: he lived with an intense bent toward initiative. Throughout Hamilton's life, his determination to take action relentlessly propelled him forward. In "My Shot," the most recognized song in Miranda's musical, Hamilton sings about not wasting his opportunities. McCarter explains that this number serves as the "I want" song. "These are the numbers that appear early in a show, when the hero steps downstage and tells the audience about the fierce desire that will propel the plot." Miranda captures, in this song, what could have been Hamilton's life mantra.

Throughout the Revolutionary War, Hamilton's initiative earned him great acclaim with many, including most importantly, George Washington. Early in the war effort, Hamilton took command of a small artillery unit. He displayed great courage, leadership, and fortitude in a number of battles. Hamilton so impressed Washington in the early months of the war that the general asked Hamilton to join his staff to provide desperately needed administrative support. Washington wrote, "At present my time is so taken up at my desk that I am obliged to neglect many other essential parts of my duty. It is absolutely necessary for me to have persons [who] can think for me as well as execute orders." Hamilton accepted this post and "took charge of Washington's staff with characteristic, electrifying speed," writes Chernow. Hamilton wildly exceeded Washington's greatest expectations, acting as his chief of staff, answering letters in Washington's name, and making decisions on his behalf. Hamilton attacked every problem that came Washington's way, overwhelming problems that threatened the very survival of the Continental Army, with his characteristic initiative.

Washington selected Hamilton to lead the American soldiers in the decisive battle of the Revolutionary War, the battle of Yorktown. With the British pinned down between American and French soldiers on land, and the French Navy by sea, Hamilton commanded the American attack that would end with the British surrender. Hamilton attacked with full force and overtook the British position in a matter of minutes. His leadership in the victory earned him a hero's status throughout America, which would prove invaluable for his future career. Hamilton's initiative played an indispensable role in America's victory in the Revolutionary War.

After the war, Hamilton focused his unrelenting initiative toward creating an effective system of government for the new union. In November of 1777, the first year of the war, the Continental Congress adopted the Articles of Confederation. These Articles functioned as the first Constitution for the United States. They were designed to give ultimate authority to the thirteen individual states, intentionally creating a weak federal government. Historian and author Joseph Ellis went so far as to say that "the government established under the Articles of Confederation was not really much of a government at all."

Washington and Hamilton had both experienced first-hand the inherent weakness of this decentralized system throughout the war. States failed to send enough troops, money, and supplies to support the Continental Army, leading to famine, disease, and crippling shortages. The lack of a strong central governing body, and the stability and accountability that such a government could provide, nearly cost America the war.

After the British surrendered, the new nation continued to operate under the Articles of Confederation. Washington and Hamilton longed to see the creation of a strong federal government to lead this new nation into its manifest destiny. Without a drastic change in the political structure, they thought the American experiment to be doomed. "Without some alteration in our political creed," Washington wrote, "the superstructure we have been seven years raising at the expense of much blood and treasure must fall. We are fast verging to anarchy and confusion."

In May of 1787, four years after American victory, Hamilton felt dismay over the lack of progress with the American government. The time for initiative had arrived. He initiated a constitutional convention in Philadelphia to discuss the challenges facing their government. During this convention, delegates proposed an entirely new Constitution, one that would replace the original Articles of Confederation. This proposal created strong debate and disagreement, and after much time spent trying to find a middle ground, the delegates finally agreed on the Constitution, in what came to be known as "The Great

Compromise." Before becoming law, however, this new Constitution required ratification by nine of thirteen special state conventions.

Countless detractors opposed the Constitution, making ratification far from certain. Opponents perceived the transition to a strong federal government as a betrayal of the values that fueled the Revolution. Many state officials, concerned about losing their power and influence to a distant federal government, threw their full weight against ratifying the Constitution. For ten months, the country debated, and the future of the United States hung in the balance. During this time, Hamilton propelled himself into the conversation, initiating an ambitious public writing campaign.

Hamilton spearheaded a project called the Federalist Papers, a series of published essays designed to build support for ratification. In a span of just seven months, Hamilton and his coauthors, primarily James Madison, produced eighty-five essays supporting the new Constitution. Hamilton wrote fifty-one of the articles, an almost unimaginable amount of writing.

The states adopted the new Constitution by a slim margin. Hamilton's unrelenting initiative shined throughout the entire process. Legal scholar James Kent writes, "Hamilton surpassed all of his contemporaries in his exertions to create, recommend, adopt, and defend the Constitution of the United States." Hamilton saw a cause he believed in and took remarkable action to ensure the outcome he desired. To idly sit back and do nothing, hoping for the best, was unthinkable for him.

When the newly elected President Washington nominated Hamilton to serve as his first Secretary of the Treasury, he knew exactly what Hamilton would bring to his cabinet. Hamilton rushed into this position with his trademark intensity. "Hamilton hit the ground running. . . . he knew the symbolic value of rapid decision making and phenomenal energy," writes Chernow.

Hamilton worked with a blank slate, and immediately began to create systems and structures for this new government. He quickly became the most influential figure in defining and shaping this new country. He created a banking and financial system from scratch, a strategy to deal with overwhelming national debt, and established tax protocol and customs regulations. In addition, he established a mail system, the beginnings of what would become the coast guard, and championed industrial advances. The breadth of Hamilton's activity during these formative years is staggering. Chernow writes, "If Washington was the father of the country . . . then Alexander Hamilton was surely the father of the American government." Joseph Ellis, in summing up Hamilton's initiative, writes, "Once Hamilton encountered a major obstacle to the advancement of any cause in which he believed, he instinctively hurled himself onto the offensive, never looked back, and waited for no stragglers. [Whatever] the objective . . . Hamilton's pattern was the same: to unleash his formidable energies in great bursts of conspicuous productivity."

Hamilton's initiative forms a major reoccurring theme throughout Miranda's lyrics. The show begins with Hamilton's friend, John Laurens, declaring that Hamilton accomplished so much because of his willingness to take initiative. Later, the entire company sings about how Hamilton always pushed forward in his life. Aaron Burr attributes Hamilton's initiative as the reason for his meteoric rise in the song "Non-Stop." Miranda recognizes Hamilton's initiative as a defining characteristic throughout his life.

* * *

Too often in my spiritual life, I lack initiative. My fear and lack of faith, in both God and myself, immobilizes me from attempting bold risks. At times, I see initiative as undermining the grace of God, as a lack of faith in God's activity and providence.

At my best, I see that grace and initiative cooperate with, rather than oppose, each other. Grace forms the foundation of our lives with God, but human initiative functions in a point-counterpoint relationship with God's grace. Both are essential for fruitful and abundant lives with God.

King David's life, and specifically his battle against Goliath, embodies this interplay between grace and initiative. God establishes David's rise by his grace, which creates new possibilities and a new future. God chooses David, an unknown shepherd boy, as the next king of Israel, not because David deserved this honor, but because of God's grace alone.

God's grace establishes the foundation of David's future. Alongside that grace, however, David takes bold and courageous initiative. David moves forward, takes risks, and places his faith in God. The interplay of grace and initiative guides, directs, and forges David's path.

Old Testament scholar Walter Brueggemann articulates this interplay: "Everything David does is derivative from and permitted by" God's presence and grace in his life. In some accounts, "David takes no initiative. He does not assert himself or express any ambition. He only receives what is given. It is all 'gift' without 'grasping.'" In other stories, however, "David is no longer a passive recipient of the actions of others. . . . Now he is assertive and prepared to take necessary and bold initiatives. . . . David does not usurp the initiative from Yahweh, but neither does he abdicate. David inquires in dutiful obedience. Then he acts according to a careful military plan."

When David enters the narrative in the Old Testament, the Israelites and Philistines were fighting in an ongoing war for land and military dominance. Israel conquered the land God promised them, but the Philistines remained entrenched in the land to the west. David's first experience of this war took place in the valley of Elah, when he brings food and supplies to his brothers who fought in Israel's army. When David arrives, the Israelites and Philistines were lined up on opposite sides of the valley, ready for battle.

A giant, named Goliath, approaches the Israelites and challenges any man to face him. None of Israel's soldiers muster the courage to face Goliath because of his imposing presence. Each day for forty days, Goliath swaggers onto the field of battle and taunts the Israelite soldiers. Each day, the Israelite soldiers cower in fear, hoping that somehow the problem will just go away. The situation had similarities to the early months of the Revolutionary War, with Washington's army in full retreat mode, terrified of their opponent.

* * *

Author Steven Pressfield, in his book *The War of Art*, writes that any time we attempt a creative act, launch a new project, or attempt anything good for ourselves or for the world around us, we face a common enemy. He names this enemy "resistance," and calls it "the most toxic force on the planet. . . . It stunts us and makes us less than we are and were born to be. . . . [I]t prevents us from achieving the life God intended when he endowed each of us with our own unique genius."

As a preacher, I come face to face with this resistance almost every week. On Monday, I begin work on my sermon. Like clockwork, by Wednesday I feel as if I have nothing of value to share with my people.

"This isn't going well," I tell myself. "You don't have anything insightful or original to say. God isn't going to use you. Prepare yourself, this is going to get ugly." The resistance I feel in those moments feels like a very real giant, wrestling me to the ground, overwhelming me with discouragement and fear.

Five years ago, I began to experiment with writing. Every time I sat down to write, resistance pulled up a chair next to me. "You aren't good enough at this—why even try?" resistance whispered. "You don't know what you are doing. You are a preacher, not a writer. Just give up now and save yourself the embarrassment of failure."

Like the Israelites, we too often give into this resistance, cowering in fear instead of taking bold initiative. We hide in rocks and in caves, hoping our problems will magically go away. We fail to walk onto the battlefield, denying the world our creative potential that offers life and blessing. God created each of us with a unique genius, with something to offer to the world. To offer that gift always requires overcoming resistance.

* * *

If Hamilton models initiative, the antagonist in Miranda's musical, Aaron Burr, epitomizes resistance. The lives of Hamilton and Burr followed a similar path. Both were orphans, fought in the Revolutionary War, practiced law afterward, and achieved successful political careers. As much as they shared in common, they were polar opposites in the issue of initiative and resistance. Miranda captures this resistance in Burr brilliantly throughout the production.

In the musical, Hamilton and his friends discuss the coming revolution and decide the time has come to take action. Burr attempts to slow them down and encourages them to keep their options open. After the war, Hamilton invites Burr to participate in the Federalist Papers project to defend the new Constitution, but Burr balks, preferring to wait and see which way the political wind will blow. If the song "My Shot" describes Hamilton's mantra, the song "Wait for It" would describe Burr's life. The lyrics describe Burr's tendency to wait and see how events would play out. As the song "Wait for It" ends, Burr intentionally pauses before singing the very last lyric, a phrasing

Miranda wrote into the script. Burr, throughout his life, seems to give into resistance at every opportunity. Miranda says, "Burr is every bit as smart as Hamilton, and every bit as gifted, and he comes from the same amount of loss as Hamilton. But because of the way they are wired, Burr hangs back where Hamilton charges forward."

* * *

When David arrives in the Valley of Elah, the situation immediately changes. He hears the taunts coming from this giant of a man across the battlefield and rages with indignation.

"Who is this uncircumcised Philistine that he should defy the armies of the living God?" David cries out. "Let no one lose heart on account of this Philistine," David tells King Saul. "I will go and fight him."

He displays incredible initiative, without losing sight of God's grace. "The Lord will rescue me from the hand of this Philistine," he declares to King Saul—who, blinded by his own lack of faith and initiative, cannot see how David, only a young boy, can possibly be serious. Resistance wins the battle with Saul.

When we get stuck in inaction, when we lack the faith and courage to take initiative, all we see are reasons why something won't work. How could this young boy possibly defeat this giant? How could I overcome the obstacles I face? Why even try? I'm just going to fail. Our creative potential rots away. We get stuck hiding in caves, defeated by resistance, unable to see anything other than impossibility.

But David defies the resistance and charges out onto the battlefield toward Goliath. He takes bold initiative while relying utterly on God's grace. "I come against you in the name of the Lord Almighty, the God of the armies of Israel, whom you have defied," David shouts. "All those gathered here will know that it is not by the sword or the shield that the Lord saves, for the battle is the Lord's, and he will give all of you into our hands."

The interplay of God's grace and David's initiative proves too powerful for Goliath. David rushes toward Goliath with five smooth stones and a slingshot, and whips his first stone through the air. It strikes Goliath on the forehead, and the battle ends as soon as it began. David cuts off Goliath's head and the Philistines flee.

We see this interplay in the New Testament as well. Paul, in his letter to the church in Corinth, writes, "But by the grace of God I am what I am, and his grace to me was not without effect. No, I worked harder than all of them—yet not I, but the grace of God that was with me." God's grace formed the foundational truth of Paul's life. His entire identity was built upon that foundation.

And yet that grace, Paul says, was not without effect. Rather, it birthed a massive amount of initiative. Paul's impact on the early church, through his missionary work and writings, is not unlike Hamilton's impact on the early American republic. He worked harder than anyone else to build upon the grace God had given him. But the moment he pointed out how hard he worked, Paul immediately jumped back to God's grace. Even the work he did, Paul said, was a result of God's grace in his life.

* * *

We far too often fail to take initiative and get stuck in caves, hiding in fear. If that describes your life today, you desperately need to take initiative, to do something. Anything really. God rarely calls us to passively observe the battles that threaten us. Many times, taking initiative, just doing something, turns the tide in our favor.

W. H. Murray writes, "Concerning all acts of initiative (and creation) there is one elementary truth, the ignorance of which kills countless ideas and splendid plans: that the moment one definitely commits oneself, then providence moves too. All sorts of things occur to help one that would not otherwise have occurred. A whole stream of events issues from the decision, rising in one's favor all manner of unforeseen incidents and meetings and material assistance which no man would have dreamed would come his way." When we move, when we overcome resistance by taking initiative, God moves with us. Our initiative creates possibilities that would never occur if we remain hiding in a cave, doing nothing.

* * *

The first six months of the Revolutionary War were an unmitigated disaster for George Washington and his Continental Army. The British invaded New York in the summer of 1776 and won every battle they faced against the inexperienced and poorly trained Continentals. Washington spent the summer and fall retreating west. In December, his army limped across the Delaware River, where they prepared to spend the winter regrouping after the humiliating and costly defeats.

Hope and faith in the American Revolution was at an all-time low. Washington's soldiers lacked food, blankets, clothing, and proper equipment. The war appeared lost as quickly as it started. Washington sensed that the outcome of the war hung precariously in the balance. "Ten days more will put an end to the existence of our army," he wrote to Congress on December 20, 1776.

The soldiers desperately needed a positive outcome to raise their spirits and belief in this war. In a surprising and daring move, Washington overcame resistance and ordered his troops to cross the Delaware River on Christmas morning, 1776, for a surprise attack on the Hessians—German soldiers hired by the British, who camped nearby.

Hamilton, bedridden with a serious illness, refused to miss the battle. He gathered his strength, willed himself out of bed, and joined the surprise attack. He crossed the Delaware River in treacherous conditions, with snow and ice pelting him, and played an important role in American's victory at Trenton, commanding a small but effective artillery unit. After their shocking victory, Washington's Army marched onward and secured another victory against the British stationed at Princeton.

Historian and author David McCullough called this moment of initiative a "great turning point" in the war. Nathaniel Greene wrote, "The two late actions at Trenton and Princeton have put a very different face upon affairs." Washington's two victories gave the soldiers hope that they could defeat the highly trained and experienced British Army. They also raised the sagging morale of Americans throughout the country, creating new momentum for the war effort. Trenton and Princeton also played a role in convincing France to enter the war—a crucial factor in America's ultimate victory.

It would have been understandable had Hamilton decided to stay in bed that Christmas Day. He must have experienced significant resistance. Many other soldiers and generals missed important battles because of illness, but Hamilton's disposition would not allow it. He could not stomach the thought of missing out. Looking at Hamilton's life, his decision was inevitable; he always chose the path of initiative.

In our lives, we must always remember God's grace, the foundation for everything we do and become. But we also must find the courage to take initiative, to overcome the resistance that opposes us in every creative act we attempt. Our initiative, no matter how small it may seem at the time, can become the great turning point in whatever battles we face.

Chapter Five

The Outsider

As an immigrant, Hamilton struggled against a steady stream of anti-outsider bias, never feeling fully accepted in America. He arrived in New York City in 1774, when thousands of immigrants flooded New York, hoping to find a better life. Many immigrants, including Thomas Paine, made an incalculable impact on their new country. Paine authored *Common Sense*, a book that stirred the colonists' revolutionary fever. Historian Gordon S. Wood describes *Common Sense*, which sold 500,000 copies by the end of the Revolution, as "the most radical and important pamphlet written in the American Revolution and one of the most brilliant ever written in the English language."

In December of 1776, as the Revolution teetered and the Continental Army hung by a thread, Paine authored *The American Crisis*, calling forth heroic commitment to the American cause. Paine wrote, "These are the times that try men's souls. The summer soldier and the sunshine patriot will, in this crisis, shrink from the service of their country; but he that stands by it now, deserves the love and thanks of man and woman. Tyranny, like hell, is not easily conquered; yet we have this consolation with us, that the harder the conflict, the more glorious the triumph."

After reading the essay, Washington ordered it to be read to his dispirited troops at Valley Forge. Paine's words inspired the soldiers and country alike, and played a critical role in the continued revolutionary effort. Paine's fingerprints, like so many other immigrants, are stamped upon the American Revolution.

When Hamilton arrived in America, he tried to forget his past and establish himself as an American insider. Chernow writes, "He chose a psychological strategy adopted by many orphans and immigrants: he decided to cut himself off from his past and forge a new identity. . . . Few immigrants have renounced their past more unequivocally or adopted their new country more wholeheartedly."

As we have seen, Hamilton impacted both the outcome of the Revolutionary War and the government of the early republic as much as, if not more than, any other Founding Father—certainly more than any other immigrant. "No immigrant in American history has ever made a larger contribution than Alexander Hamilton," writes Chernow.

Yet no matter how far reaching his impact, no matter how honorably he served the early republic, Hamilton never rose above the stigma of being an immigrant. This reality constantly hounded him, both internally and externally. His many political opponents would never allow him to lose sight of it.

The insults John Adams spewed at Hamilton, "bastard brat of a Scotch peddler," "Creole bastard," and "the foreigner," exemplify the vitriol Hamilton endured. Adams considered Hamilton, as a foreigner, incapable of understanding the true American spirit. Adams wrote that Hamilton "could scarcely acquire the opinions, feelings, or principles of the American people." Adams' wife, Abigail, shared her husband's opinions, suggesting that "a more careful and attentive watch ought to be kept over foreigners."

As Hamilton's power and influence grew, so did the anti-immigrant bias against him. Chernow writes, "People would assume that Hamilton, as an 'outsider' or 'foreigner,' could not possibly be motivated by patriotic impulses. Hence, he must be power mad and governed by a secret agenda."

Miranda captures this anti-immigrant bias throughout the musical. Hamilton's political opponents, James Madison, Aaron Burr, and Thomas Jefferson, lament about Hamilton's growing influence in their new country. As they discuss Hamilton, they don't even call him by name, simply referring to him as "the immigrant." Later, they accuse him of using his position as Secretary of the Treasury to embezzle money from the US Government. Because of his immigrant status, they threaten him and suggest he leave the country and go back home.

Hamilton's enemies do not see him as a real person, as a human being with inherent value. They don't see him for who he is; they only see an immigrant, an outsider. They place him inside a clearly defined box. This refusal to accept him as a valued member of America communicates that he doesn't belong, simply because of his place of birth.

* * *

Hamilton's status as an immigrant, and the subsequent abuse he experienced, raises a relevant question for our lives today: How are we, as followers of Jesus, to treat the outsider? The church must grapple with this question. At this moment in history, it presents one of the most pressing issues we face.

The current refugee crisis, the greatest since World War II, demands a faithful response from the church. At the end of 2015, more than 65 million people had been forced to leave their countries, one out of every two of these refugees being children. Violence and unrest forces 34,500 people from their homes every day. I watched a documentary on this crisis in shock and disbelief at the images that flashed across my television screen: apartment buildings and schools blown in half, children covered in blood as they wailed in hospital rooms, desperate families fleeing violence and terror. Images of a three-year-old Syrian boy who washed up onto a beach shocked the world. He had drowned while fleeing his home with his family for a better life in Europe. These refugees experience an almost-unimaginable amount of violence, horror, and death. This refugee crisis cannot be ignored.

* * *

One Sunday after church, our community hosted a piano recital in our sanctuary. In the back of the room, the group running the recital placed a donation box for Kansas City refugees. The sixty people who attended the recital donated thirteen dollars. While I love the heart of those who wanted to help refugees in our city, only a select few dug into their pockets for a little extra cash and tossed it into the box. Nobody made a real sacrifice, planned ahead to give a significant gift, or gave anything that actually hurt. They gave, rather, out of convenience. The image of that donation box unsettled me, and later that week, God convicted me of this truth: that donation box reflects how I treat the outsider.

I don't live with open disregard of immigrants in our country, like Adams or Hamilton's other political opponents. But I'm also not making any real sacrifice to help refugees. I'm not giving time or emotional energy to help relieve the plight that thousands of immigrants in my city experience daily. Anything that I do give, I give out of convenience.

I made an effort to love the outsider once. My wife and I sponsored an immigrant who lived in our city, named Prem, through Catholic Charities. We committed to simply being his friend, inviting him into our lives, and helping him with practical needs. That summer, we sporadically spent time with Prem. We brought him to the zoo with our family, invited him to a party we hosted, and had him over for dinner a few times.

One afternoon, I taught Prem how to drive a car. We practiced in his apartment parking lot for a few hours. I asked if he wanted to try driving on a real street, and he eagerly said yes. In retrospect, it was an extreme lack of judgment on my part.

Prem slowly drove toward the parking lot exit, where a stop sign encouraged him to come to a complete stop before he pulled out onto the road. Apparently, I hadn't explained stop signs when we practiced in the parking lot, which now seems like a slight oversight. He rolled toward the stop sign, then through it and into the street as another car barreled toward us at forty miles per hour. At the last possible second, I reached over and grabbed the gear shifter, slamming the car into park. Our car stopped, and the oncoming car swerved around us. I looked at Prem, who appeared visibly shaken, and suggested to him that we switch seats so I could drive back into the parking lot. He quickly agreed.

After a few months of sponsoring Prem, Allison and I called Catholic Charities and told them we couldn't continue the relationship. Our lives were too busy, and the relationship wasn't convenient. The friendship required too much of our time and energy, so we walked away. We ended our "sponsorship" almost five years ago, and I have done embarrassingly little since that halfhearted effort when it comes to loving the outsiders among us.

* * *

Jesus models a radical love and acceptance of the outsider. In the world Jesus inhabited, Jews and Gentiles each formed one predominant category of "insider" and "outsider." Many Jewish people considered Gentiles unclean pagans who threatened their holiness code. Jews avoided contact with Gentiles, refused to share meals with them, and worshipped in separate areas in the temple to avoid contamination.

Jesus, however, shattered these categories between Jew and Gentile, between insider and outsider—a truth Donald Kraybill powerfully articulates in his book *The Upside Down Kingdom*. Kraybill highlights a number of different stories in the Gospels that emphasize Jesus' radical acceptance of the outsider.

In the Gospel of Luke, Jesus launches his preaching ministry in his hometown of Nazareth. On the Sabbath, Jesus stands up in the local synagogue and shares an Old Testament story about the prophet Elijah, whom God sent to a Gentile woman—rather than to a Jewish household—in a time of famine. From the outset of his ministry, Jesus declares that his calling includes all peoples, rejecting any category that separated insider from outsider. This claim so incensed the Jewish crowd that they attempt to throw Jesus off a cliff.

Jesus performs many miracles in Gentile land, including the second miraculous feeding of the multitude, where Jesus multiplies the bread and fish. Jesus uses seven loaves, and afterward, the disciples gather seven baskets of leftovers. Throughout the Scriptures, the number seven represents completeness, wholeness, and perfection. The kingdom of God, this story communicates, finds completion when outsiders are welcomed to the table.

In another story from the Gospel of Matthew, Jesus shares a meal with outsiders, tax collectors, and sinners. The Jewish religious leaders object, and Jesus' response leaves no doubt that he intends to shatter their carefully constructed boxes: "I'm here to invite outsiders, not coddle insiders."

Kraybill observes, "The spirit of Jesus penetrates social boxes. Barricades of suspicion, mistrust, stigma, and hate crumble in his presence. He calls us to see the human beings behind stigmatized social labels. His kingdom transcends all boundaries. He welcomes people from all boxes. His love overpowers the social customs which divide, separate, and isolate."

* * *

The Old Testament offers a similar perspective, consistently calling the Jewish people to love the alien, stranger, and outsider living among them. In Leviticus, God gives various commands to Israel to flesh out the Ten Commandments. "When a foreigner resides among you in your land, do not mistreat them. The foreigner residing among you must be treated as your native-born. Love them as yourself, for you were foreigners in Egypt. I am the LORD your God."

God commands Israel to love the outsider. In Scripture, love never represents only an emotion, but rather a call to specific, tangible action or sacrifice on behalf of another. Too often we think of obedience to God in terms of behaviors we should avoid. This passage reminds us that obedience involves our engagement with God and others as much as our avoidance of sinful behavior.

New Testament scholar Samuel E. Balentine writes, "Holiness must be manifest in lives that say both yes to what God requires and no to what God forbids. One without the other will never be sufficient to obey God's commandments. . . . Holiness must always be exemplified by *active engagement* with the world, never only by *passive withdrawal.*"

God unleashes great redemptive power when we love the outsider with tangible action. Thomas a Kempis writes, "Love is a mighty power, a great and complete good; love alone lightens every burden, and makes the rough places smooth. It bears every hardship as though it were nothing, and renders all bitterness sweet and acceptable."

God commands us to love the outsider. Can you remember the last time you obeyed that command? The last time you loved an outsider with a practical, tangible, concrete act of service? I'm ashamed to say that the last time I obeyed this command was teaching Prem how to drive, all those years ago.

God calls Israel to love the outsider, because they were once outsiders in Egypt. He encourages them to remember the difficultly of living among a people that was not their own. The Egyptians spoke a different language, had different culture and customs, viewed the Israelites with suspicion, and treated them as insignificant. The Egyptians placed the Israelites in a box, refused to see beyond the label of outsider, and oppressed them for generations. They shared the hostility Hamilton's opponents felt toward him. Remember what that felt like, God says, so that you might offer compassion and love to others who find themselves in a similar situation.

* * *

Israel's history as outsiders in Egypt reminds us of our history in the kingdom of God, where all of us stood as outsiders at one time. Paul writes to the church in Ephesus, "As for you, you were dead in your transgressions and sins, in which you used to live when you followed the ways of this world and of the ruler of the kingdom of the air, the spirit who is now at work in those who are disobedient. . . . But because of his great love for us, God, who is rich in mercy, made us alive with Christ even when we were dead in transgressions—it is by grace you have been saved."

Every one of us were outsiders—far from God, dead in our sins. But God, because he loves us more than we can possibly begin to imagine, sent his Son, who gave us life. God, by his grace, transformed us from outsider to insider. How quickly we forget that truth—just as many outsiders can begin to see themselves as insiders, forgetting the suffering that outsiders experience.

* * *

The longer Hamilton lived in America, the less tolerance he showed toward other immigrants. He once wrote that William Findley and Albert Gallatin, two immigrant government officials, "were both foreigners and therefore not to be trusted." This strange reversal in his attitude toward immigrants betrayed his own immigrant past. Chernow writes, "Findley, who had been born in Ireland, found it scandalous that Hamilton of all people should object to his immigrant background: 'I say for secretary Hamilton to object to such a man as a foreigner must be astonishing to those who have any knowledge of his own history.'" Chernow continues that later, Hamilton "predicted that 'the influx of foreigners' would 'change and corrupt the national spirit,'" and spoke out again against the foreign-born Gallatin: "Who rules the councils of our own ill-fated, unhappy country? *A foreigner!*" How quickly we who were foreigners in Egypt, once outsiders ourselves, forget that experience and consider ourselves insiders.

* * *

Author Ann Voskamp models for us a faithful response to the current refugee crisis. Her family sponsored a refugee family that moved to her hometown for an entire year, providing financial, emotional, and practical support. She helped this family find a home, solicited furniture donations, and set up a swing set in their backyard. She helped enroll the children in a local school, where they took English as a Second Language classes and participated in the school play. Voskamp gave her life to these outsiders and challenges others to follow her example, to practice what she calls "cruciform hospitality"—hospitality in the shape of the cross.

Voskamp says, "The church has always been for the stranger, the sojourner, always been the welcoming arms of the Savior. How can we not move heaven and earth to let the fleeing refugees in, when heaven moved and he came to earth to let us in?" This decision to practice cruciform hospitality will cost us greatly. Voskamp continues, "It's relatively easy to pontificate on how to live the gospel, it's infinitely harder to incarnate the gospel in your own life."

* * *

My friend David faithfully practices this cruciform hospitality. Called by God to befriend the immigrant community in Kansas City, he moved into a neighborhood populated by immigrants and outsiders. He built relationships with his new neighbors and practiced hospitality.

He quickly identified friendship as their greatest need. David remarks, "Loneliness is the underlying issue. What they need is a genuine friend. . . . Their core struggle is feeling alone, abandoned, pushed out, rejected. All of those lies, their journey has been telling them . . . you can attend to that deepest need very easily by simply being a part of their lives."

In his book *Strangers Next Door,* author J. D. Payne shares stories of immigrants, and the same theme of friendship emerges. He tells the story of Jo, who came to the United States six years ago, looking for a better life for his family. He hoped to find a job that could provide financially for his large family, and an education for his children. "What I found," writes Jo, "was twelve hour workdays and very little time with my children." He worries his children will forget who they are and where they came from. "Very few people have befriended us. . . . We are so lonely here. Where is our hope? Who will be our friend?"

Fatima arrived five years ago, with her eleven children, after war in her home country took her husband's life. "Before coming to this country, we spent many years in a refugee camp in another country near our home. Life there was very hard. We had little food, and there was no schooling for my children." They arrived in America, "completely lost and lonely. My knowledge of the language is still poor. We all still have nightmares about the things that happened in our own country. We also fear what will happen to us here in this new country. How will we survive? Does anyone care?"

May is an international student at a university. "Taking classes in a different language is very hard. It is also difficult to be separated from my family. In my country, three generations of a family usually live together in one house. Here at the university, I live by myself. Most of the time, I am lonely. I want to get to know some nationals, but everyone seems so busy and like they are in such a hurry. Does anyone care? Who will be my family while I am here?"

* * *

Hamilton struggled with this same loneliness when he came to this country. Toward the end of the war, he experienced several rejections, failing to win nominations for political positions he hoped to receive. He wrote in dejection, "I am a stranger in this country. I have no property, no connections." Hamilton wrote these words almost seven years after he came to America. He had just married Eliza and been welcomed into her prominent family. He built a number of close friendships. Yet his words expose the hard and lonely reality that outsiders struggle to overcome.

My friend David hopes to alleviate some of this pain and loneliness by building friendships with outsiders in his neighborhood. He tries to teach his children about the importance of this calling. One night, he read *The Lion, the Witch, and The Wardrobe* to his daughter. During the scene where the wardrobe becomes a portal to a different world, his five-year-old daughter interrupted him.

"Daddy, what is a wardrobe?" she asked.

"It's kind of like a closet," David replied.

"Our closets aren't like that," she lamented.

"You're right, our closets aren't like that," he told her. "But our kitchen table is."

David believes that sitting at his table with an immigrant or outsider causes a kingdom portal to open up. One night, an

Iraqi refugee, a homeless man, and an ex-addict all sat around his table, sharing spiritual conversation. His table transformed into a portal, ushering them all out of the hard and lonely reality they had come to know, and into the experience of feeling welcomed and accepted. David's kitchen table ushered them into the presence and love of God.

* * *

We can experience this reality in our lives if we commit to cruciform hospitality, offering costly acts of love to the outsider among us. God commands us to live this way. And deep down, we really do care about the poor, the vulnerable, the outsider among us.

In one scene from *Hamilton*, Hamilton and the Marquis de Lafayette, a French military officer, discuss their plan for the battle of Yorktown. At one point, the two outsiders look at each other and rap about how immigrants can be counted on to get things done. The audience erupts after this line at every performance. Miranda and his team decided to add two extra bars of music after that line, because the crowd always missed the next two lines of dialogue. They were too busy affirming the truth that had just been spoken.

We really do care about the outsider. My friend David now leads a community of close to fifty Americans who moved into the same neighborhood as his family. Stirred by David's example, they live a life of cruciform hospitality alongside of him. We care about the outsider because God created us in his image, and God cares deeply about the poor, the vulnerable, the outsider. We simply have to start living what we already care about. We have to practice cruciform hospitality, opening our lives and our hearts to the outsider among us. When we do so our tables, and our very lives, transform into a portal that ushers the outsider into the kingdom of God.

Chapter Six

Sinner and Saint

A brilliant, passionate, and driven man, Hamilton's extraordinary strengths enabled him to impact the early American republic as much as any other Founding Father. An administrative genius, he brought organizational order and structure out of chaos in his various roles within the military and new government. He served the country with integrity and honor, displaying strong personal character. In establishing a system for national finances, Chernow describes Hamilton as "an American prophet without peer," operating with a greater understanding of financial systems than almost every one of his contemporaries. He worked tirelessly and devoted himself to whatever task required his attention. The breadth and contents of his writings reveal a bright intellectual mind and a relentless drive to accomplish his goals.

He possessed many relational strengths as well, building a number of close friendships. He loved Eliza and his children deeply, once writing to Eliza, "I need not add that I am impatient to be restored to your bosom and to the presence of my beloved children. 'Tis hard that I should ever be obliged to quit you and them. God bless you my beloved. . . . Yours with unbounded affections, A. Hamilton." Chernow remarks,

"Hamilton wrote dozens of such tender notes to Eliza. Whatever his imperfections, he was a caring father and husband who often seemed anxious about the health and welfare of his family. . . . His love for [Eliza] . . . was deep and constant if highly imperfect." Hamilton accomplished an incalculable amount of good, both in his public career and in his private life.

Yet Hamilton also possessed substantial flaws. At times he lacked self-restraint, discipline, and displayed a serious lack of judgment. His pride contributed to a falling-out with Washington during the Revolutionary War, as Hamilton left his staff for a time. He grievously betrayed his wife in his affair with Maria Reynolds and subsequent publishing of the Reynolds Pamphlet. He alienated most of the Founding Fathers at one time or another. His duel with Burr seems now a logical outcome of his unyielding personality. "What kind of a guy was Hamilton?" asks historian Joanne Freeman, "To a lot of people a lot of the time, he was an arrogant, irritating asshole." Many times, even his strengths morphed into flaws, depending on circumstances. Miranda observes, "His inability to shut up, his tenacity, his drive, they are all great strengths in the war. But in the absence of a common enemy, that virtue goes inward, and they go from assets to flaws."

Chernow sums up the contrast in Hamilton: "Charming and impetuous, romantic and witty, dashing and headstrong, Hamilton offers the biographer an irresistible psychological study. For all his superlative mental gifts, he was afflicted with a touchy ego that made him querulous and fatally combative. He never outgrew the stigma of his illegitimacy, and his exquisite tact often gave way to egregious failures of judgment that left even his keenest admirers aghast. If capable of numerous close friendships, he also entered into titanic feuds with Jefferson, Madison, Adams, Monroe, and Burr." Hamilton truly was a mixed bag, possessing both significant strengths and destructive flaws.

The Founding Fathers shared this truth with Hamilton. These men accomplished extraordinary triumphs, leading our country into revolution and defeating the most powerful army in the world. They transitioned from a violent revolution into a peaceful, democratic form of government, which proved no easy task. They embodied courage, vision, tenacity, and brilliant intellect. Joseph Ellis calls them "the greatest generation of political talent in American history." British philosopher Alfred North Whitehead considered the time during which these men led, along with Caesar Augustus' Rome, as the two greatest eras of political leadership in all of western history.

But these Founding Fathers also possessed significant flaws and experienced tragic failures in their lives and leadership. As they fought the war, huge mistakes driven by ego or poor judgment almost cost them victory. While debating the structure for the new national government, they could hardly get along, publishing scathing essays in local newspapers. One failure towers above all others: their inability to address and end the brutal reality of slavery, which will forever stand as the greatest moral failure of our country's history.

Most of the Founding Fathers owned slaves, including Washington and Jefferson. Jefferson, who wrote "All men are created equal" in the Declaration of Independence, betrayed this basic belief. Author Joseph Ellis writes,

> The darkest shadow is unquestionably slavery, the failure to end it, or at least to adopt a gradual emancipation scheme that put it on the road to extinction. Virtually all the most prominent founders recognized that slavery was an embarrassing contradiction that violated all the principles the American Revolution claimed to stand for. And virtually every American historian who has studied the matter has concluded that the persistence and eventual expansion of slavery made the Civil War almost inevitable.

Miranda's musical captures this moral failure. Jefferson first appears in the musical, Miranda explains, "descending a staircase with our ensemble scrubbing the floors and getting his bags. It's the paradox of Jefferson made flesh: The writer who articulated liberty so clearly was an active participant in the brutal system of slavery." During the last number of the production, Eliza sings about how Hamilton would have continued to fight slavery if he had lived longer. As Eliza sings about this, "Washington, bows his head in shame. It's [Jackson's] way of having Washington accept responsibility for what he did and didn't do," writes McCarter.

Author and historian Annette Gordon-Reed encourages us to acknowledge both sides of these men's lives. She observes, "There were great things that were done, there were terrible things that were done. The best thing to do is to see both of them." Senator Elizabeth Warren agrees, "These are not perfect people. They are deeply flawed people. But they made contributions. You have to see both." Miranda says *Hamilton* communicates this paradox, "Our show does a good job of reminding us that all of us are more than one thing."

Ellis powerfully articulates the presence of both strengths and flaws in these men's lives: "Taken together, these triumphal and tragic elements should constitute the ingredients . . . [of] a storyline rooted in the coexistence of grace and sin, grandeur and failure, brilliance and blindness." This idea resonates deeply within me because it describes my life. My life is rooted in the coexistence of grace and sin, grandeur and failure, brilliance and blindness. I struggle mightily with learning how to accept both sides.

* * *

Martin Luther once wrote the Latin phrase *Simul Justus et Peccator*, which means "simultaneously saint and sinner." Our lives with God, Luther realized, exhibit the same coexistence of grace and sin, grandeur and failure, brilliance and blindness that Ellis observed in the Founding Fathers. Both realities exist inside of us at the same time. This might seem contradictory. How can we be both sinner and saint simultaneously? Author F. Scott Fitzgerald guides us down the path: "The test of a first-rate intelligence is the ability to hold two opposed ideas in mind at the same time and still retain the ability to function." Living an abundant spiritual life depends on our ability to hold both of these seemingly opposed ideas, that we are sinners and saints, in our minds and hearts at the same time.

* * *

We see this truth throughout the life of Peter, Jesus' most colorful disciple. Peter experienced both significant triumphs and heartbreaking tragedies, often from one moment to the next. Peter's life, like the Founding Fathers, displayed the coexistence of grace and sin, grandeur and failure, brilliance and brokenness. Author George Lyons writes, "Peter's character, as presented in the Gospels . . . is remarkably consistent: He could be depended upon to be inconsistent."

One night, Jesus sends his disciples across the Sea of Galilee while he remains behind to pray. In the middle of the night, a figure approaches the disciples' boat. Overwhelmed with terror, they believe the figure to be a ghost. Then they recognize Jesus' voice calling out to them, "Take courage! It is I. Don't be afraid."

Peter responds immediately: "Lord, if it's you, tell me to come out to you on the water." Jesus invites Peter out onto the water, and Peter, in a moment of tremendous courage and faith, steps out into the sea, walking on top of the water. What a triumph! He risks so much in faith and experiences the miraculous power of God in his life.

But then Peter takes his eyes off Jesus and notices the wind and the waves all around him. Immediately he begins to sink and cries out, "Lord save me!" Jesus catches and then chides him. "You of little faith, why did you doubt?"

Peter's triumph turned into failure in an instant. He displays great faith in one moment, then doubt overwhelms him in the next. He climbs back into the boat feeling embarrassed and ashamed. Triumph and tragedy coexist for Peter in this remarkable story.

Later, Jesus gathers his disciples around and asks them about his identity. Peter responds, "You are the Messiah, the Son of the living God." Jesus offers high praise to Peter, declaring that God himself had revealed this truth to him.

In the very next passage, Jesus predicts that he will be arrested, suffer, and ultimately die a shameful death. Peter takes Jesus aside and rebukes him. Jesus' response is swift and harsh, "Get behind me Satan! You are a stumbling block to me; you do not have in mind the concerns of God, but merely human concerns." Peter experiences a devastating failure, completely misunderstanding Jesus' call as the Messiah. From triumph to tragedy in the blink of an eye.

Later, as Jesus approaches his passion, he predicts that his disciples will abandon him. Peter professes his undying loyalty. "Even if all fall away on account of you," he declares, "I never will." That evening, Roman soldiers arrest Jesus and bring him to trial. Peter follows them to the courtyard of the high priest. Three times people accuse Peter of being one of Jesus' disciples; three times Peter denies knowing Jesus. In the courtyard, Peter's weakness, fear, and self-concern lead him into his greatest failure.

Peter's life offers us a storyline rooted in the coexistence of grace and sin, grandeur and failure, brilliance and brokenness. Author W. D. Davies observes that Peter's life exhibits a "jarring juxtaposition." I love that phrase, because it gives language to the reality I experience in my life every day.

* * *

We must learn to acknowledge the reality of both sinner and saint, because each perspective anchors us in an important truth about ourselves and life with God.

Remembering that we are sinners drives us to humility. We live each moment with a deeper reliance on God's grace. This perspective keeps us from pride and self-righteousness, and reminds us that we need God's grace every single moment of our lives.

Jesus tells a story about two men who come to the temple to pray, a Pharisee and a tax collector. The Pharisee thanks God that he was not like other "sinners." He brags about his life of religious discipline, feeling quite proud of himself.

The tax collector, however, stands at a distance, unable to even look up to heaven. He begs God, "God, have mercy on me, a sinner." Jesus shocks his listeners by telling them that the tax collector, rather than the Pharisee, went home justified before God. Recognizing his sinfulness drove the tax collector to humility and dependence upon God.

Washington embodied this humility and acknowledgement of mistakes during his farewell address, published after his decision to step down from the presidency after his second term. It reads,

> Though, in reviewing the incidents of my administration, I am unconscious of intentional error, I am nevertheless too sensible of my defects not to think it probable that I may have committed many errors. I shall also carry with me the hope that my country will view them with indulgence and that after

forty-five years of my life dedicated to its service with an upright zeal, the faults of incompetent abilities will be consigned to oblivion, as I myself must soon be to the mansions of rest.

Miranda observes Washington's recognition of his weaknesses and flaws in these words, a theme he incorporates throughout his musical. He writes, "In [his farewell address], Washington seeks to do exactly what we aim to do with this musical: paint himself as human, and capable of mistakes."

When we acknowledge our sinful nature, we admit our inexhaustible capacity for failure and mistakes. Instead of allowing that acknowledgement to rob us of our inherent value, we must simultaneously offer compassion to ourselves. "Be kind to yourself," my mentor often reminds me. To be flawed is human. God recognizes this truth and accepts us as we are, flaws and all.

A number of times during script meetings, Miranda's team asked questions about Hamilton's flaws. McCarter writes, "Is the flawed, historically accurate Hamilton too unsympathetic? Were his failures . . . alienating the audience?" I struggle with these same questions in my life. Too often I feel as if my flaws, failures, and mistakes will alienate others, and even God. I think my flaws render me unworthy of being loved and accepted.

Javier Munoz, who took over the lead role of Hamilton after Miranda stepped down, believes the opposite. He believes that Hamilton's flaws actually draw people into his story. "[Hamilton's flaws] allow the audience to say, 'I'm okay the way I am—flawed and human.' It pulls them in closer."

Tommy Kail, the director of *Hamilton*, gave the cast freedom to make mistakes at their very first rehearsal. He believed mistakes would lead to new insights for the entire production, and "new discoveries, new mistakes" became a daily mantra. How much freedom would we find if we accepted our flaws and realized mistakes lead to new discoveries of God's unconditional love? What if we saw our failures as opportunities to learn and grow—opportunities to dive further into the grace of God?

Repeating the words from the Jesus prayer, "Lord Jesus Christ, Son of God, have mercy on me, a sinner," helps me to move closer to this freedom. During the first half of the prayer, "Lord Jesus Christ, Son of God," one inhales, breathing in God, his presence, and his grace. The second half of the prayer, "have mercy on me, a sinner," reminds me that I am a sinner, but that Jesus will have mercy on me. Exhaling during this phrase helps us to release and breathe out all of our failures and disappointments. This prayer offers a powerful discipline in the journey toward accepting my sinfulness, while offering myself compassion.

* * *

Remembering that we are saints requires reimaging. Nelson Mandela says, "I am not a saint, unless you think of a saint as a sinner who keeps on trying." Thomas Merton suggests that being a saint has very little to do with us, and everything to do with God. "A saint is not someone who is good but who experiences the goodness of God."

Using these helpful redefinitions, all of us qualify as saints. When we claim this truth, we recapture our inherent goodness. God created each of us in his image; therefore, so much good exists inside each of us. When we remember that we are saints, we fight back against the insecurity, the disappointment, even the self-hatred that we feel.

Paul writes to the church in Ephesus, "For we are God's masterpiece." Out of all of God's creations, human beings represent his crowning achievement—a truth we easily forget. Richard Rohr says, "Our job is to remind people of their inherent goodness."

I struggle to believe in my inherent goodness. I look at my life and often feel like a failure, like I'm always going to struggle, that I'm never going to become the person God created me to be. I live at times with deep disappointment and imagine God feeling that disappointment as well. In these moments, remembering that we are saints can free us. Remembering that God created us in his image, that we are God's masterpiece, helps us to move from disappointment to genuine self-acceptance.

* * *

Out of all of the flawed, broken characters we find in *Hamilton*, Aaron Burr stands above the rest. He plays the villain, both in the musical and in our history of the Founding Fathers. The build-up to the duel between Hamilton and Burr offers insight into his character and Hamilton's chief accusation against him.

Burr and Hamilton had been political opponents for more than fifteen years, experiencing a number of harsh disagreements. Hamilton perceived Burr as a man fundamentally lacking in character, willing to switch political allegiance and principles, depending on what benefited him personally. In Hamilton's mind, Burr posed a real threat to the integrity of the new nation. Ellis writes, "Character mattered because the fate of the American experiment with republican government still required virtuous leaders to survive." Hamilton's criticisms of Burr were "a realistic response to the genuine vulnerability of the still-tender young plant called the United States. So much seemed to be at stake because in truth, it was."

Hamilton confronts Burr's lack of character in "Your Obedient Servant," the song before their duel, asserting that Burr only thinks about himself. Ellis agrees with Hamilton's assessment of Burr, "Burr, if I have him right, is the odd man out within the elite of the early republic, a colorful and intriguing character, to be sure, but a man whose definition of character does not measure up to the standard." Irony exists in Burr's lack of character, as his grandfather was the great American theologian and preacher Jonathan Edwards.

Burr's behavior leading up to his duel with Hamilton casts him in a particularly bad light. Stories surfaced, after he shot and killed Hamilton, about him taking target practice in the weeks before the duel. Burr seemed to be fine-tuning his marksmanship, with many contemporaries believing that Burr went into the duel with the definite intention of killing Hamilton. After Hamilton's death, Burr was charged with murder, compared to Benedict Arnold by newspaper editors, and fled to the South in disgrace, his political career and reputation forever ruined.

Burr falls squarely in the category of sinner, and yet goodness existed in him as well. He served honorably in the Continental Army, rising to the rank of colonel and receiving a commendation from Congress. He advocated for women's rights and fought to abolish slavery. He appears to have been a kind and loving father to his daughter, Theodosia. Although he had significant flaws, at times genuine goodness flowed out of him and into the world. The line between sinner and saint became blurred at times, as it does in all of us.

The song "Dear Theodosia" captures this blurring of lines. Sung by Burr and Hamilton, the song illustrates how much villain and protagonist share in common. They both were orphaned at a young age, served their country honorably in the war, and longed to see their young country grow into its enormous potential, although they had very different ideas about what that meant. They both also loved their children, and sing the same words to them during "Dear Theodosia," promising to give everything they could to help them come of age and thrive. At the end of the song, the two characters sing in unison. The line between hero and villain, sinner and saint, is completely blurred. Their song tells the story of the coexistence of grace and sin in all of our lives.

* * *

Flannery O'Connor, an American writer in the mid-1900s, wrote a prayer journal in her twenties. In it, she describes her spiritual struggles, "I will always be staggering between despair and presumption." We fall into despair when we lose sight of the truth that we are saints. We struggle with presumption when we forget that we are sinners. O'Connor acknowledges both truths throughout her journal.

She writes about her failures, her weakness, and her sinful nature. "Dear God," she writes, "I cannot love Thee the way I want to. You are the slim crescent of the moon that I see and my self is the earth's shadow that keeps me from seeing all of the moon. . . . I do not know You God because I am in the way." In another passage she writes, "Mass again . . . has left me unmoved—thoughts awful in their pettiness & selfishness come into my mind even with the Host on my tongue." Her journal closes on a discouraging note, "My thoughts are so far away from God. He might as well not have made me. . . . Today I have proved myself a glutton—for Scotch oatmeal cookies and erotic thought."

And yet her goodness and desire for God shines through as well. "Please help me to get down under things and find where you are," and "I want so to love God all the way. . . . I don't want to be doomed to mediocrity in my feeling for Christ. I want to feel. I want to love. Take me, dear Lord, and set me in the direction I am to go." Even the very act of writing a prayer journal sets her apart as a saint, as one who pursues God and experiences his goodness. O'Connor lives simultaneously as sinner and saint. Throughout her journal she acknowledges and accepts the presence of both truths.

* * *

In talking about the character of George Washington, Miranda articulates the challenge of making his characters real.

"It is so important to take George Washington off the pedestal. These were real people who lived and died. I think one of the things we really tried to do with the show is show them all as flawed. There's no saints in this show, not one."

I don't entirely agree. Sinners fill his show, deeply flawed characters whose failures and brokenness saturate the story with tension and conflict. But *Hamilton* is also filled with saints, saints who are deeply flawed. In truth, that is the only kind of saints we have.

Chapter Seven

Equality

The America Hamilton knew was marred by gross inequality. Women faced an uphill battle in the recognition of their rights. Hundreds of thousands of people of color lived a brutal, dehumanizing existence as slaves. Miranda's musical challenges us to wrestle with the inequalities people faced in that era, and the inequalities that still remain entrenched in our culture today.

People believed women were inferior to men during the Revolutionary era. Married women could not own property, vote, or hold political office. The women's suffrage movement wouldn't even begin for another fifty years. Single women held slightly more legal rights than married women, but those rights were rescinded once they entered into marriage.

Author Carol Berkin, in her book *Revolutionary Mothers*, writes about the prevailing perspective on the place of a woman in society. "Chief among a woman's truths was that God had created her to be a helpmate to man and Nature had formed her for this purpose. Her natural inclination was to obedience, fidelity, industriousness, and frugality and her natural function was bearing and nurturing children." Men considered women weaker and inferior to their sex, with education offering one example. "The lingering belief that the female brain was too weak to absorb abstract ideas barred them from all but the most elementary education," writes Berkin.

Many women of this era accepted this subordination as truth. In 1742, Eliza Lucas Pinckney wrote, "[I am] making it the business of my life to please a man." Martha Washington's "only motive was a sense of duty," writes Berkin, "for as a wife she believed herself bound to accede to her husband's wishes." Martha once wrote about joining her husband at camp during the war, "[If] he will send for me . . . I must go."

Miranda challenges historical assumptions about gender in *Hamilton*. In one scene, Angelica sings about how the only expectation for her is to marry a rich man. Yet Miranda's characters push the traditional boundaries. New York theatre Director Emma Miller suggests, "When we're introduced to Hamilton's soon-to-be wife Eliza Schuyler and her sisters Angelica and Peggy, we meet three women who are fluent in philosophy and politics and who speak out about their place in early American society. . . . From the outset, we know these women aren't going to be sitting politely on the sidelines of history."

If women faced an uphill battle in their fight for equality, people of color found themselves in an all-out war. Slaveholders considered slaves their property, oftentimes treating them worse than livestock. Slaveholders whipped, hanged, beat, and branded their slaves. Female slaves were raped and sexually abused.

Many colonists, including Hamilton, fought for the freedom of slaves. They considered slavery a stain on the national soul and a contradiction of the values of the American Revolution.

Abigail Adams wrote, "It always seemed a most iniquitous scheme to me, to fight ourselves for what we are daily robbing and plundering from those who have as good a right to freedom as we have."

Hamilton fought against slavery as an abolitionist for years, helping create an organization in New York that eventually ended the institution of slavery in the state. Author James Oliver Horton writes, "[Hamilton] was one of those who refused to ignore the illogic, the irreligious, the hypocritical racial distinction that many of his friends and associates in Revolutionary America were willing to make. He publically condemned Americans who demanded freedom for themselves as a God-given right, while depriving others of freedom and profiting from that deprivation." Hamilton refused to believe in the idea of people of color as inherently inferior to others, writing, "for their natural faculties are as good as ours."

Miranda portrays the struggle of racial inequality throughout the show, and his decision to cast the Founding Fathers as people of color brings the conversation of race to the forefront. Chris Jackson says, "By having a multi-cultural cast, it gives us, as actors of color, the chance to provide an additional context just by our presence onstage, filling these characters up." Miranda's musical challenges all of us to wrestle with the question of gender and racial inequality today.

* * *

For the early church, the question of equality quickly turned into a central defining issue. The church began in Jerusalem, where Jesus' death, resurrection, and ascension took place. The disciples received the Holy Spirit on the day of Pentecost, and a number of Jewish people responded to Peter's preaching about Jesus.

But the gospel quickly spread to the Gentile world, primarily through the apostle Paul's ministry. Tensions developed between the Jews and Gentiles, as they struggled to relate to one another. The Jewish people understood themselves as God's chosen people and had for centuries lived under the Torah, God's laws that prescribed holy living. Many Gentiles did not recognize the Torah and didn't feel the gospel required them to submit to Jewish law. Some Jews resented this stance. At times, the Jewish people's attitudes and actions toward Gentiles made them feel less than the Jews, as if they were second-class citizens. Inequalities began to infiltrate the early church.

Paul confronted Peter on this issue, in an account found in his letter to the Galatians. While in Antioch, Peter shared table fellowship with Gentile Christians. The practice of sharing meals was a significant issue in the question of Jew and Gentile relationships. Many conservative Jews refused to share table fellowship with Gentiles, as the Torah declared strict food laws— laws which Gentiles didn't observe. Conservative Jews feared that sharing a table with Gentiles would expose them to foods that would render them ritually unclean.

Peter, the leading figure of the Jerusalem church, took a more liberal stance in Antioch. He shares table fellowship with the Gentiles, believing that Jesus' gospel message of unity and acceptance took precedence over the purity laws in the Torah. This decision to share table fellowship was monumental. N. T. Wright says, "It's hard for Westerners today to see how serious a matter table-fellowship was in the early church. . . . Eating with people is one of the most powerful symbols of association. . . . [I]t involved the very heart of the gospel." Sharing table fellowship in the early church offered a powerful symbol of unity, acceptance, and equality. New Testament scholar George Lyons writes, "Shared meals demonstrated mutual trust, loyalty, and solidarity."

After Peter establishes the habit of table fellowship, "certain men from James" come to Antioch, and Peter "began to draw back and separate himself from the Gentiles," because of his fear of these men. We can assume these "men from James" were conservative Jews who didn't believe Jews should be associating with Gentiles. The presence of these men compels Peter to draw back from table fellowship. Scholars believe Peter had good reason to be afraid. George Lyons writes, "Jewish zealots threatened violence on Jews who failed to comply with the laws maintaining the boundaries between Jews and non-Jews, such as circumcision and kosher laws. . . . Josephus reported a massacre of thousands of Jews during Passover of AD 49 as a result of an uprising instigated by Zealots. This was probably at about the same time Peter was in Antioch."

Peter's withdrawal does not stem from superficial concerns about what others think because he shares table fellowship with Gentiles. Rather, Peter possibly fears for his very life. These men from James could have come to Antioch specifically to target

Peter as the leader of the new church, engaging in the quite liberal practice of sharing table fellowship with Gentiles.

Paul confronts Peter about this issue, because for Paul, Peter's withdrawal contradicts the very heart of the gospel. If sharing table fellowship communicated unity and equality, drawing back from that fellowship communicated the opposite, threatening the message of the gospel. Imagine how the Gentiles felt when Peter, and other Jews with him, pulled back from table fellowship. They must have felt less than the Jewish Christians, suffering the sting of inequality. This struggle threatened the unity and equality of the new movement.

Later in his letter to the Galatians, Paul articulates the truth that Peter violates, "So in Christ Jesus you are all children of God through faith, for all of you who were baptized into Christ have clothed yourselves with Christ. There is neither Jew nor Gentile, neither slave nor free, nor is there male and female, for you are all one in Christ Jesus."

Paul communicates here a radical statement, given his cultural context. His culture assumed male superiority over females and Jewish superiority over Gentiles. Author Scot McKnight references a Jewish blessing prayed daily by some Jews: "Blessed be God that he did not make me a Gentile . . . blessed be God that he did not make me a woman." Donald Kraybill writes, "It's difficult for us to grasp the meager status in Hebrew culture of women, stashed at the bottom of the heap with slaves and children."

Paul challenges those assumptions, suggesting that in Christ, "there is neither Jew nor Gentile, neither slave nor free, nor is there male and female." Instead, "oneness in Christ Jesus" now defines the life of the early church.

Author Richard Hays writes, "If the church is to be a sign and foretaste of the new creation, it must be a community in which gender distinctions—like the ethnic and social distinctions . . . have lost their power to divide and oppress. This does not mean that those who are in Christ cease to be men or women. . . . Rather, it means that these distinctions are no longer the determinative identity markers, no longer a ground for status or exclusion."

McKnight agrees, "[This passage announces] the irrelevancy of one's social status for acceptance with God and life in the church. As with culture or race, so with social status: there are distinctions but they are irrelevant."

Hamilton possessed a similar vision of oneness for America. He acted as one of the primary forces that forged the early republic together into one unified and equal nation. He hoped that the union would be "constantly assimilating, till they embrace each other, and assume the same complexion." Hamilton's vision for America sounds quite like Paul's vision for the early church. I like to imagine, although I admit a bit of conjecture, that Paul's call to oneness and equality in Galatians influenced Hamilton's thinking and vision for what these thirteen different states might become.

* * *

The church has struggled, like Peter in Antioch, to live out this equality throughout its history. George Lyons quotes Saint

Augustine, who in the fifth century "acknowledged that Paul's idealistic vision of oneness in Christ had not yet been fully achieved within the church." Augustine writes, "Difference of race or condition or sex is indeed taken away by the unity of faith, but it remains embedded in our mortal interactions."

The church continues to struggle with this today. We have made significant progress with issues of race and gender, yet too often women and people of color still struggle against inequalities.

As we've already seen, people in the first century assumed the inferiority of women. Scot McKnight writes, "Women were talked about in rude and condescending ways; they were not to be taught the law; they were to tend to their children; they were not considered reliable witnesses in court; they may have even sat in seats separate from men in synagogues." Significant strides have occurred since that time, but the belief in the inferiority of women persists today. Makers.com, a platform fighting for women's rights, shares harrowing statistics about inequalities women face. Women earn around seventy-seven percent of their male counterparts' earnings; African-American and Latina women earn even less, sixty-four percent and fifty-six percent respectively. Sixty-two million girls are denied an education throughout the world. Four out of five victims of human trafficking are girls. Women currently hold less than five percent of CEO positions at S&P 500 companies. Thirty percent of women who have been in a relationship report that they have experienced some form of physical or sexual violence by their partner. Female genital mutilation (FGM) affects more than 125 million girls and women today.

In case you think these issues remain outside the church, Lyons writes about the injustice and sexism within the church. "In the U.S., my female students divinely called to ministry must be at least twice as good as their male counterparts to be seriously considered as pastoral candidates."

This sexism explicitly betrays the example of Jesus. Jesus honored women, allowed them to follow him as his disciples, and considered them as equals to men. Kraybill writes, "[Jesus'] treatment of women implies he views them as equal with men before God. In a stunning upheaval, he declares that female harlots will enter the kingdom of God before righteous Jewish males. The prominence of women in the Gospels as well as Jesus' interaction with them confirms his irreverence for sexual boxes. He doesn't hesitate to violate social norms to elevate women to a new dignity and a higher status." We must, as followers of Jesus, confront any attitudes or behaviors that exhibit inequality for women—a stance that directly contradicts both Jesus' example and Paul's writings.

* * *

People of color continue to struggle against inequalities as well. In a fascinating book by Tanner Colby, *Some of My Best Friends are Black*, Colby traces how the history of the city I live in, Kansas City, was built upon deliberate, deceitful, and racist actions that perpetuated inequalities for people of color.

J. C. Nichols developed a large part of Kansas City. He invented the concept of the all-white neighborhood, which made him a very rich man. He developed neighborhoods around Kansas City, which contained restrictive covenants that kept people of color out. Colby writes, "J. C. Nichols didn't sell houses. He sold 'suburbia.' He sold a way of thinking about residential living that in turn created the demand for houses in neighborhoods that he owned."

Central to the neighborhoods Nichols developed was the promise of "desirable associations." Nichols' actual property deeds read: "None of said land may be conveyed to, used, owned, or occupied by negroes as owners or tenants." Nichols was the first developer to apply racial covenants to entire neighborhoods.

White America considered Nichols' developments genius. Four different US presidents appointed him to serve on national commissions for planning developments. But Nichols' idea of suburbia clearly communicated and established entrenched structures of inequality. Whites began to draw back and separate themselves from people of color, fleeing to the "desirable associations" of the suburbs, in what we now call "white flight."

Colby gives a harrowing history of race inequality and even abuse in the American church. He describes rural parishes in the 1700s in New Orleans, where "colored parishioners typically sat in separate pews at the rear or on the side of the church. They also had to go to communion last, after whites. And in no parish were people of color allowed to participate in the liturgy; they could not become priests or hold any meaningful position in the church hierarchy."

Colby points out how these inequalities continue today. Sunday morning at 10 o'clock continues to be the most segregated hour in America. Many small towns have two separate Catholic churches, one white and one black. Many times, the parishes sit across the street from each other. He tells the story of Wallace Belson, who in 1964, wandered into the wrong Catholic church. "Upon seeing a black man enter, two white men left their pews, went over, and confronted him in the vestibule. Then they started beating him. Right there in church. Dropped him to the floor, kicked him in the head, the back, again and again, then threw him out the door and down the steps into the parking lot below. All of this took place while the other congregants sat in their pews and looked on, saying and doing nothing."

Some progress has been made since the 1960s, but we have a long way to go in the fight for racial equality. McCarter writes about how the *Hamilton* cast recognizes their role in this struggle. One day during rehearsal, as the cast rehearsed "One Last Time," a song sung by Chris Jackson as Washington, the cast heard about the racially motivated killing of nine worshipers at Emanuel AME Church in South Carolina. Jackson said the violence "stopped him cold," and reminded him of how far we still have to go.

* * *

I struggle with knowing how to respond to the inequalities that exist in our culture and the church today. These issues have entrenched themselves in the church since its inception. Solving them feels overwhelming and complex; I simply do not know what to do.

Colby shares a story of William Stringfellow, an Episcopalian theologian who spoke at the Conference on Religion and Race in Chicago in 1963. "He savaged Catholics and Protestants alike for lending four hundred years of moral sanction to slavery and segregation. He pointed his finger at every last preacher in the room, including himself. They were to blame— *they* had done this. He derided the efforts of the conference as being 'too little, too late, and too lily white.' Stringfellow's solution? He didn't have one. 'The most practical thing to do now,' he said, 'is weep.'"

Weeping, mourning, and confessing the ways we have perpetuated inequalities feels like an appropriate first step. And yet we must do more. What would it look like to lean into the problem of sexism and racism in the church today? Whereas Peter drew back and separated himself from the Gentiles, how might we lean in and practice unity with people who have experienced the injustice of inequality? Leaning in captures Christ's desire for his church, a truth Paul writes about in his letter to the Ephesians: "For he himself is our peace, who has made the two groups one and has destroyed the barrier, the dividing wall of hostility. . . . His purpose was to create in himself one new humanity out of the two, thus making peace."

Leaning in and wrestling with the problems of inequality requires reimagining. Perhaps Miranda's greatest act of reimagination in his entire production was his decision to cast people of color as the Founding Fathers. This decision challenges the audience to question long-held assumptions and break out of their normal ways of thinking. It also offers an alternative narrative for people of color in our country, including Daveed Diggs, who played Thomas Jefferson in the original Broadway cast. Diggs said that seeing *Hamilton* as a kid might have changed the entire trajectory of his life. "A whole lot of things I just never thought were for me would have seemed possible," he said. Bill Coulter, a teacher from Brooklyn, whose class attended *Hamilton* through the generosity of the Theatre Development Fund, asked his students how watching actors of color play the Founding Fathers affected them. They told him how proud they felt, and how seeing the actors of color in *Hamilton* gave them a sense of belonging in this country.

What might happen if each of us reimagined our responsibility in the fight against inequality? If we challenged our long-held assumptions about race and gender? My friend Jake, who worked at a ministry for seven years in Kansas City's urban core, says the solution begins with awareness. "Look for ways that you participate in inequalities. It is your problem. Don't make assumptions. Hear what people are saying. Listen to them." He suggests that all of us unknowingly participate in oppressive, systematic inequalities. As a white male suburbanite, I live in ignorance about the ways I contribute to this reality. Out of sight, out of mind. To counteract this ignorance, each of us has to participate in and reimagine the solution for the church to embody oneness and equality for all.

* * *

New Testament scholar Richard Hays shares a story where the church embodied this call to equality. "In 1994 [in Rwanda], members of the Hutu tribe carried out mass murders of the Tutsi tribes. At the town of Ruhanga, fifteen kilometers outside of Kigali, a group of 13,500 Christians had gathered for refuge. They were of various denominations: Anglicans, Roman Catholics, Pentecostals, Baptists, and others. According to the account of a witness to the scene, 'When the militias came, they ordered the Hutus and Tutsis to separate themselves by tribe. The people refused and declared that they were all one in Christ, and for that they were all killed,' gunned down en masse and dumped into mass graves."

These martyrs gave their very lives to embody the truth that we all are one in Christ. Their sacrifice witnesses to us and demands a reimagining of how we might stand as one against the inequalities that people face in our world today.

Chapter Eight

Forgiveness

In Philadelphia during the summer of 1791, an attractive twenty-three-year-old woman named Maria Reynolds approached Hamilton's front door. She knocked and requested to speak privately with him about an important, personal matter. Although a stranger to Hamilton, he invited her inside. Hamilton recounted Maria telling him about her husband, James Reynolds, "who for a long time had treated her very cruelly, [and] that lately left her to live with another woman and in so destitute a condition that, though desirous of returning to her friends, she had not the means."

Hamilton, never one to turn down someone in need, offered assistance to Maria. He sent her home and promised to bring some money later that evening. When he arrived at her house, Maria led him inside and invited him into a bedroom. Rather than giving her the money and returning home to his wife, Hamilton gave into temptation, beginning an affair that would have disastrous consequences on his family, reputation, and political career.

Shortly after that fateful evening, Eliza and their children left town for a summer vacation in Albany with her parents. With his family out of town, the affair intensified. Hamilton met with Maria frequently that summer, with many of their meetings happening at Hamilton's own house.

James Reynolds, after learning of the affair, demanded blackmail money for the wrongs Hamilton committed against him. Hamilton, terrified that Reynolds would expose him, paid him various sums throughout the affair. Shockingly, Reynolds encouraged Hamilton to continue the relationship, provided he continue to pay for his wife's services. Hamilton's decision to continue this affair under these circumstances offers one example of his gross lapses in judgment. Chernow calls Hamilton's behavior "one of history's most mystifying cases of bad judgment."

Three Republican legislators, including James Monroe, obtained information about Hamilton's payments to James Reynolds. They accused Hamilton of speculation, of using his government position for personal profit, and threatened to bring the information to Washington. Hamilton confessed the affair and subsequent blackmail to his interrogators, who agreed to keep Hamilton's secret—as his relationship with the Reynolds represented a personal, rather than a public, matter.

The affair remained a secret for almost five years, until a disreputable writer, James Callender, published a series of pamphlets, accusing Hamilton of speculation and the extramarital affair. Chernow writes, "Once Callender's charges were published, Hamilton faced an agonizing predicament: should he ignore the accusations as beneath his dignity or openly rebut them?"

Hamilton's friends encouraged him to remain silent, suggesting the scandal and accusations would eventually lose steam. Hamilton, whom Chernow suggests was "incapable of a wise silence," decided against their advice. Instead, Hamilton responded to Callender by publishing a pamphlet of his own, known as the Reynolds Pamphlet. In it, he proclaimed innocence in regard to the charge of speculation. He had always conducted his role as Secretary of the Treasury with the highest integrity. His real crime, which he fully confessed in intimate detail, was committing adultery with Maria Reynolds, and subsequently submitting to blackmail by her husband. Hamilton wrote, "The charge against me is a connection with one James Reynolds for purposes of improper pecuniary speculation. My real crime is an amorous connection with his wife, for a considerable time with his privity and connivance." Hamilton's affair with Maria, exposed by his own published response, became the first ever government sex scandal in the history of our country.

Hamilton's opponents pounced, astounded by his foolishness in publishing a response. Even his friends responded with disbelief and questioned his judgment. Other contemporaries pitied Hamilton and his shameful behavior. "Alas, alas, how weak is human nature," wrote Abigail Adams in response to the scandal.

One can only imagine Eliza's humiliation and shame as her husband deceived and betrayed her in the worst possible way. To make it worse, he publicly exposed his own infidelity, bringing shame upon his entire family. He had broken a promise he had made to Eliza years earlier, writing to her, "Indeed my angelic Betsey, I would not for the world do anything that would hazard your esteem. 'Tis to me a jewel of inestimable price &

I think you may rely I shall never make you blush." Author and historian Tilar Mazzeo, who read some of Eliza's letters that survived, offers insight into Eliza's emotional state: "After the affair, Eliza felt depressed, unwanted, and irrelevant."

Presumably, Eliza couldn't stand to be in his presence. She travelled to Albany to stay with her parents for a season and to give birth to her sixth child while Hamilton stayed behind in New York. He found himself exposed, alone, and without the woman he most loved in the world. In other words, he found himself in the exact same place we all end up far too many times in our lives: in desperate need of forgiveness.

* * *

We need forgiveness because of our flawed, broken, and imperfect nature as human beings. We want so badly to do the right thing, to live with integrity, to love people well. But we continually come face to face with our inability to do so. We yell at our kids, tell half-truths, and say hurtful things about others. We give into addictions, deceive ourselves, and cheat on our spouse and pay blackmail to keep it under wraps. All these wrongs leave us with a constant, gnawing sense of regret, guilt, and shame—for the hurt we caused, and for our failure to love.

Psalm 130 articulates this desperate need for forgiveness. "Out of the depths I cry to you, LORD; Lord, hear my voice. Let your ears be attentive to my cry for mercy. If you, LORD, kept a record of sins, Lord, who could stand?"

The psalmist finds himself in the depths—a rich image throughout Scripture that describes the chaos that too often overwhelms our lives. Author James Luther Mays writes that Psalm 130 "discerns the human situation. Life is lived in danger of, and also in the experiences of, 'the depths'. . . . It represents drowning in distress, being overwhelmed and sucked down by the bottomless waters of troubles." Such is life.

The psalmist arrives in the depths because of his sin. He acknowledges his brokenness, failure, and inability to live the life God created him to live. He displays an impressive honesty in this psalm, refusing to blame God for the chaos that overwhelms his life. He recognizes the truth that his sin and failures are responsible for the chaos. He shudders to think what would happen if God held his sins against him.

"If you, LORD, kept a record of sins, who could stand?" the psalmist asks. The short answer, of course, is no one. If God kept a record of our sins, we would remain stuck in the chaos, trapped forever in our sin, guilt, and shame. And stuck not only with our internal guilt, but also with the external consequences of our brokenness and selfishness. "It is not just guilt," writes Mays. "It is the flood of wrong and its consequences that sweeps life along and from which there is no escape apart from a liberating, rescuing redemption."

* * *

The first few verses of Psalm 130 describe the chaos that Hamilton must have felt when he realized the full extent of his transgressions against Eliza. Can you imagine his regret, shame, and even self-hatred? In an unpublished essay Hamilton wrote months later, Hamilton offers a confession of the cost of his adultery. Chernow writes, "[Hamilton] reiterated his faith in marital fidelity and his knowledge that adultery damaged families and harmed the adulterer as well as the deceived spouse." Hamilton experienced this damage firsthand, from the chaos that crashed in around him, as he found himself drowning in the depths.

Miranda's team captured this chaos masterfully during the song, "The Reynolds Pamphlet." Intense lights flash, music erupts out of the speakers, and the dancers just go crazy, personifying the chaos.

This visual representation of chaos captures our experience, epitomizing how we feel whenever we come face to face with our own inexhaustible capacity for wrongdoing. Is there any hope for us? Is there a way forward? Is there a way out of the chaos and the depths?

Too often, when confronted by these questions, we believe the answer to be no. In our heads, we know that God promises to forgive us. But actually believing, accepting, and living out that forgiveness proves elusive. Guilt and shame overwhelm us and seem to override the forgiveness and grace of God. We believe that because we have failed so egregiously, God will not forgive. Hamilton surely doubted whether he could ever be forgiven, by both Eliza and God.

* * *

One of my sons went to school on his twelfth birthday, excited to celebrate with his friends. His day got off to a bad start in gym class. He didn't listen to his teacher and spent the hour in the hallway. He wept when his homeroom teacher picked him up. "I'm a loser," he said. "I'm worthless. I'll always be this way."

My son had failed; he had made a mistake. Although not listening to a teacher seems innocent enough to us, from his perspective he came face to face with his brokenness. At that moment, he could not even dare to believe in the possibility of forgiveness. His teacher shared the story with me a week later. Her eyes filled with tears as she described the level of shame my son felt. I wonder if her emotion came from a recognition of the struggle to believe in the possibility of forgiveness.

Thankfully, the psalmist opens up new possibilities for us. He cries out from the depths, overwhelmed by the consequences of his sin and brokenness. Yet he dares to believe that God remains with him, his mercy still available. "But with you, there is forgiveness, so that we can, with reverence, serve you."

The psalmist displays great courage and faith in his understanding of God. Brueggemann says, "the prayer is an act of inordinate boldness." Oftentimes, we lack this boldness; we cannot imagine a God who remains with us in our failure, brokenness, and sin. Too often, we live as if the depths will have the final word. The psalmists offer us hope. When it appears that the depths have swallowed us up, with no future possibility, the psalmist declares the forgiveness of God. In this moment, this glorious moment, God's forgiveness rescues us from the depths, and transports us to a place of hope, of future, of possibility.

With God, there is always forgiveness—not because he has to forgive, but because he longs to forgive. Lewis Smedes asks, "Does God forgive us because he is pressed by some law that obligates him to forgive? Or does he forgive because something inside bends him toward grace instead of revenge? God is not obligated by anything outside his own heart. He forgives because he wants to. And he wants to because he knows that the possibilities for the future are much brighter for both of us if he says yes to forgiving."

God forgives because whereas all you can see in the depths are your failure, your brokenness, and your imperfections, God looks at us and sees our future. He looks at us and sees his original intention. He forgives us, because every time he offers us forgiveness, he offers yet another chance for us to become the person he created us to be.

One of the most important questions we will ever wrestle with is whether or not we will accept God's forgiveness. Can we leave behind the shame, the guilt, and the humiliation we feel about our brokenness and sin? Can we believe and live out the truth that God forgives us? Forgives us because he loves us more than we can even begin to imagine? Forgives us because he longs to open up future possibilities for our lives with him? Will we accept this forgiveness, and walk boldly into a new future that forgiveness alone makes possible?

* * *

God calls us to do more than simply accept his forgiveness. After we experience forgiveness from God, he challenges us to offer that same forgiveness to others who have wronged us.

In Jesus' parable of the unmerciful servant, a king decides to settle his accounts. One servant owes him a fantastic sum of money, and the king orders him and his family to be sold to pay back the debt. The servant begs the king for mercy, asks for patience, and promises to pay back everything. The king knows that the debt is unpayable. Scholars estimate he owes the king the equivalent of a billion dollars today, an amount a servant could never repay. The servant finds himself in a hopeless situation, with no future and no way forward.

The servant represents our reality before God. We have wronged, dishonored, and sinned against him. We owe him a debt we can never repay.

The story, however, takes an unexpected turn. The servant's master cancels his debt, offering forgiveness! New hope, new possibilities, and a new future emerges out of the depths.

The servant goes out in this newfound freedom and encounters a fellow servant who owes him a small amount of money. He grabs him and chokes him, demanding this servant pay back what he owes. This servant begs for mercy. "Be patient with me," he cries, "and I will pay it back."

You might think this scene would bring back a recent memory for the servant who has just been forgiven his debt. Yet he refuses the other servant's request and throws him into prison until he can pay back the debt.

The king hears about this servant's behavior and calls the servant back into his presence. "You wicked servant," he says. "I canceled all that debt of yours because you begged me to.

Shouldn't you have had mercy on your fellow servant just as I had on you?"

This parable confronts us with the same question: Shouldn't we have mercy on others, just as God offers mercy to us? Accepting forgiveness from God proves difficult, but it might be even harder to forgive others. "Forgiveness," Phillip Yancey says, "is an unnatural act." It goes against everything we want when we are wronged. C. S. Lewis agrees, suggesting that "Everyone says forgiveness is a lovely idea, until they have something to forgive." Imagine how hard forgiveness would have been for Eliza. Hamilton betrayed, deceived, and publically shamed Eliza and their entire family to save his political reputation. How does someone forgive such an act?

During the utter chaos in the song "The Reynolds Pamphlet," Eliza stands just off stage preparing for her next song. She stands quietly, alone, off to the side, as the chaos erupts all around her. Phillipa Soo, who played Eliza in the original Broadway cast, said that watching the chaos offstage made her think about how Eliza felt after reading her husband's pamphlet. She wears a white gown that emphasizes her innocence during the next song. The audience wonders, will Eliza find it within her to forgive?

* * *

Smedes shares a story that illustrates how difficult offering forgiveness would have been for Eliza. A man met a young homeless woman, and convinced his wife to welcome her into their home. The wife prayed about the situation and saw an opportunity to serve and bless a young woman in desperate need. She never considered that the arrangement might tempt her husband.

One day, she came home early from the gym and walked in on her husband and this young woman having sex in their living room. She immediately threw them both out of the house. Months later, the wife continued to wrestle with her response to this betrayal. As a Christian, she knew God called her to forgive, but she couldn't bring herself to actually do it. "I've heard it all my life, we should forgive people who slam us. But now when it happens to me, I don't have a clue what it is I'm supposed to do." She said that she would rather buy a gun and shoot them both than forgive.

President Bill Clinton's public affair gives us more insight into Eliza's struggle to forgive. Like Hamilton, Clinton's affair turned into a government sex scandal at the highest level, for the entire country to witness. Bill deceived Hillary for months as the rumors of his affair grew. He finally told her the truth the night before he confessed in front of a grand jury.

"I could hardly breathe," writes Hillary, "Gulping for air I started crying and yelling at him. 'What do you mean? What are you saying? Why did you lie to me? I was furious and getting more so by the second. . . . I was dumbfounded, heartbroken and outraged that I'd believed him at all. . . . I wanted to wring his neck."

When someone feels deeply wronged, forgiveness seems like an impossibility. We have all faced situations where we knew we were called to forgive someone, but didn't know how we could.

In those moments, forgiveness seems so unfair and violates our sense of justice.

Philip Yancey points out that we have only two options when someone wrongs us: forgiveness or vengeance. The path of revenge is so tempting. We love the idea of paying someone back for the wrong they committed. But this path transforms us into a prisoner to the person who committed those wrongs. This path fills our hearts with bitterness, anger, sorrow, and pain. Throughout the history of humanity, we've seen that this path can never lead to healing or wholeness. It simply leads to more hurt, pain, and unforgiveness.

When we choose the path of forgiveness, we find freedom. The Greek word for forgiveness found throughout the New Testament speaks to this truth. Yancey suggests that this word is so much more robust than our English word forgiveness. "The most common Greek word for forgiveness means, literally, to release, to hurl away, to free yourself." When we forgive someone else, we are letting go, releasing, hurling away the wrongs committed against us. We free ourselves from our hurt, bitterness, and rage. Smedes writes, "The first and often the only person to be healed by forgiveness is the person who does the forgiving. . . . When we genuinely forgive, we set a prisoner free, and then discover that the person we set free was us."

Hamilton wronged his wife deeply, causing an unimaginable amount of shame and humiliation. Eliza must have struggled to forgive her husband and rebuild their marriage. Author Tilar Mazzeo points out that the Hamiltons had numerous children throughout their marriage, but in the years after the affair, a long gap existed between their children. It appears they struggled to rebuild intimacy and trust after Hamilton's betrayal.

In the song "Burn," we witness Eliza's inability to offer forgiveness to Hamilton, at least initially. The song's title is based on Eliza's decision to burn the letters she wrote to Hamilton over the years while he was absent from her. Her decision to burn these letters offers a window into the pain Eliza felt over this betrayal. This collection of love letters would have been one of Hamilton's most treasured possessions. She deprives him of her words of affection and love in this act. She hurts him in the deepest way she knows how. In the song "Burn," Eliza sings about her hurt, sense of betrayal, and the hate she feels toward her husband.

Yet Eliza walked deeply with God and ultimately forgave her husband. The scene of Eliza forgiving Hamilton—which, appropriately, takes place in a garden—provides one of the most powerful moments in the entire musical. Hamilton and Eliza stand together onstage, and Hamilton tries to reconcile their relationship. Eliza's face is hard, her body language tense, she shows no response to Hamilton's pleadings. But then, in a moment, she softens. Her face moves from anger to sadness. She reaches out and grabs Hamilton's arm, and begins to sing with him.

I like to imagine Eliza wrestling with God over this issue of forgiveness. She must have felt so hurt and betrayed by her husband, yet she still loved him and knew God called her to forgive. I wonder if Eliza read the parable of the unmerciful servant and reflected on how much God had forgiven her throughout her life. I like to imagine that this parable helped Eliza offer forgiveness to her husband.

She forgave Hamilton, and, in that act, found freedom. She went on to live a remarkable life, fighting against slavery, raising money for the Washington monument, working on her husband's biography, and establishing the first private orphanage in New York City. Forgiving Hamilton made this life possible. Her forgiveness created a new future, with new hope and new possibilities, not only for their marriage but for herself as well. She lived a life that would have been impossible had she been shackled by the chains of unforgiveness. The forgiveness she offered her husband set her free to spend her energy not on bitterness, hatred, and revenge, but on offering grace and love to a broken world.

Eliza models for us God's call to forgive. When we follow Eliza's example of forgiveness, we find freedom, love, and life. We create a new future filled with possibility, opened up by forgiveness and forgiveness alone.

Chapter Nine

Despair

The last years of the 1700s ushered Hamilton into a season of intense despair and depression. Having struggled with depression from time to time, Hamilton found himself in new depths during this terrible season. Three different events in Hamilton's life crashed down on him in these few years, reducing him to a shadow of his former self.

In 1795, Hamilton resigned from his position as Secretary of the Treasury. Working for the government paid well below what he could have earned practicing law; Hamilton had become indebted and needed to improve his financial situation. He wrote, "I am not worth exceeding five hundred dollars in the world. My slender fortune and the best years of my life have been devoted to the service of my adopted country. A rising family hath its claims."

After resigning, he enjoyed a good relationship with George Washington and continued to influence government policy and practice. Hamilton's Treasury successor, Oliver Wolcott Jr., regularly sought advice from Hamilton on department decisions. Hamilton's influence weakened when Washington stepped down after his second term and John Adams became the next president. When Washington left the presidency,

Hamilton lost his greatest advocate and friend within the US government.

Adams and Hamilton shared a mutual distrust and dislike. The two leading figures of the Federalist party simply could not get along. Adams' cabinet still looked to Hamilton for direction—a reality Hamilton hid from Adams. When Adams discovered Hamilton's stealth influence, he was understandably furious and fired the cabinet members still loyal to Hamilton.

Four years later, Thomas Jefferson defeated Adams and Hamilton's political position worsened. His greatest political opponent now held the position of highest power, and Hamilton quickly found himself a political outsider. Chernow writes, "Once Jefferson became president, Hamilton, forty-six, began to fade from public view, an abrupt fall for a man whose rise had been so spectacular, so incandescent. . . . Hamilton had shown a steady knack for being near the center of power. He had gravitated to Washington's wartime staff, the Confederation Congress, the Constitutional Convention, and the first government. Now he was exiled from the main political action, a great general with no army marching behind him." This loss of influence and power must have been a crushing defeat to Hamilton, a man who for almost three decades found himself at the very center of the American republic.

Hamilton's affair with Maria Reynolds and subsequent decision to publish the Reynolds pamphlet contributed to his depression. One can imagine a volatile and painful season of marriage, as Alexander and Eliza attempted to reconcile after his unfaithfulness. The pain that his infidelity caused Eliza, the woman he loved so deeply, no doubt drove him even deeper into despair.

Yet another disaster, the most excruciating of all, struck Hamilton's life in 1802. That year, his eldest son, Philip, was shot and killed during a duel of honor. Philip, almost twenty at the time, was a handsome and bright young man. He graduated with high honors at Columbia College, and the Hamilton family had high expectations for Philip's life. "Hamilton regarded Philip as the family's 'eldest and *brightest* hope' and was grooming him for major accomplishments," writes Chernow.

A passionate, pro-Republican speech given by George Eacker at a Fourth of July celebration in New York City ignited the confrontation. In the speech, Eacker disparaged Hamilton and the Federalists, and credited Jefferson, the Republican president, for saving the Constitution. Philip burned with indignation about Eacker dishonoring his father's name and challenged him to a duel, which he accepted.

Duels of honor were common in this era, and seen as a noble way to defend one's honor in the face of conflict. Most men reconciled before reaching the point of violence, and even when a duel actually occurred, rarely would a participant be mortally wounded. Joseph Ellis writes, "Just as most duels in this era did not end in death or serious injury, most negotiations over matters of honor did not end in duels." If two men did end up on the dueling grounds, a shooter typically tried to glance their opponent's arm or leg, the point being to wound rather than kill. In this particular duel, Philip and the Hamiltons would not be so fortunate.

Before the duel, Philip discussed dueling etiquette with his father. Hamilton encouraged his son to intentionally shoot his weapon into the air, an actual dueling technique called the *delope*. When this occurred, it was assumed that the duel would end, with each participant retaining their sense of honor.

Philip followed his father's advice, hoping to end the duel without injury. Eacker, however, took aim at Philip, striking him above his right hip. The wound took Philip's life; he died early the next morning. Before he passed, Philip professed his faith in Christ and made his peace with God.

Imagine the regret and remorse that flooded Hamilton's mind. Philip's desire to protect his father's honor drove him to the dueling ground in the first place. Then, the advice of shooting into the air failed his son and led directly to his death. Hamilton must have felt fully responsible for the death of his beloved son. Chernow writes, "Having been abandoned by his own father, Hamilton must have regretted keenly his failure to protect his son."

After Philip's death, grief overwhelmed Hamilton and his family. Chernow writes, "Eliza was inconsolable. . . . Angelica (Philip's sister) was so unhinged by his death that she suffered a mental breakdown. . . . Hamilton tumbled into a bottomless despair." Hamilton's friend, Robert Troup, wrote, "Never did I see a man so completely overwhelmed with grief as Hamilton has been." Hamilton himself wrote that Philip's death was "beyond comparison the most afflicting of my life."

In a few short years, Hamilton had fallen from the second most powerful position in the country to political exile, betrayed his wife and exposed her to public humiliation, and lost his firstborn and dearly loved son. Despair and depression understandably overwhelmed his life.

A lyric from the song "It's Quiet Uptown," powerfully captures the Hamilton's despair after Philip's death. In the song, Angelica sings about unnamable suffering and the temptation to simply give up when despair overwhelms us. This song powerfully captures our response when despair assails our lives.

* * *

We all know the experience of despair. We have all suffered through seasons where the circumstances of our lives seemed hopeless. A marriage failed. A relationship fell apart. We lost a job or found ourselves in a dead-end career. We pursued an opportunity, took a real risk, and it didn't pan out. Failure crushed our dreams.

I am quite familiar with despair, having gone through two seasons of clinical depression. During these seasons, ministry circumstances overwhelmed me so completely that I saw nothing but defeat, discouragement, and darkness. In those seasons, I felt this darkness would last forever. I remember struggling to get out of bed in the morning, let alone holding onto hope throughout the day.

Much more common in my life are the day-to-day experiences of despair: the failures, disappointments, and discouragements that quickly morph into despair. I get into an argument with my twelve-year-old son, give a consequence, and he responds by saying he hates me. I give into temptation yet again. A family that I've invested significant time in decides to leave our church. Despair assaults our lives almost daily.

Andy Blankenbuehler, the choreographer of *Hamilton*, knows this despair intimately. While he worked on choreographing Miranda's musical, his five-year-old daughter battled cancer. For two years, she underwent chemotherapy. The despair he experienced during that time found its way onto the stage. McCarter writes, "The way that the 19 actors moved . . . was, in some ways, a reflection of what one man was suffering. . . . Andy knew what it was like 'when someone you love is dying and they're in your arms.'"

* * *

The author of Psalm 42 experienced a deep despair that made its way into his art as well, in this case not a musical, but a poem written to God. "My tears have been my food day and night. . . . Why my soul, are you downcast? Why so disturbed within me? . . . I say to God my Rock, 'Why have you forgotten me? Why must I go about mourning, oppressed by my enemy?' . . . Why my soul, are you downcast? Why so disturbed within me?"

The psalmist offers a poignant image later in this psalm. He writes, "Deep calls to deep in the roar of your waterfalls; all your waves and breakers have swept over me."

The psalmist mentions Mount Hermon earlier in the psalm, possibly referring to the several different peaks in a mountain range located on Israel's northern frontier. A number of different streams come together in this region to form the Jordan

River. During the rainy season, the streams burst with water, creating powerful waterfalls that cause massive flooding down the mountain, destroying everything in its path.

The psalmist offers this image of "waves and breakers sweeping over me," to describe his experience of despair. Imagine cascading, crashing water rushing down a mountain. The psalmist imagines himself standing on the slopes of the mountain as the floods sweep over him. This captures the overwhelming reality of despair.

When we face this torrent of despair in our lives, it is so easy to give up hope. When we feel like we are sinking, drowning, and overwhelmed by the depths, it is hard to fight against the current.

The psalmist offers another possibility. At the same time that the psalmist feels utterly overwhelmed by despair, he refuses to give up hope. Overwhelmed by despair, he does not give into it. "Why, my soul, are you downcast? Why so disturbed within me? Put your hope in God, for I will yet praise him, my Savior and my God." In the face of despair, the psalmist clings to hope and refuses to let go.

* * *

As the leader of the Continental Army, George Washington had more reason to despair than most. He led poorly trained and undisciplined soldiers, who lacked equipment, proper clothing, blankets, and food. They constantly faced hardships from the elements and more than half of the Continental soldiers who died during the war were killed by disease. Soldiers refused to reenlist at critical moments, and generals often worried more about their rank and ego than the good of the Army. In addition to the struggles within his Army, he faced the most powerful enemy in the world, superior in numbers, artillery, and experience. Despair hounded him constantly. Washington writes, "I believe I may, with great truth, affirm that no man perhaps since the first institutions of armies ever commanded one under more difficult circumstances than I have done." William Hooper, a North Carolina delegate who signed the Declaration of Independence agreed, "Oh how I feel for Washington. . . . The difficulties which he has now to encounter are beyond the power of language to describe."

Yet one of Washington's greatest strengths—a strength Hamilton was intimately acquainted with as his aide-de-camp—was his ability to not give into despair. General Schuyler wrote Washington about the overwhelming troubles and difficulties that faced his men. Washington replied, "We must bear up against them, and make the best of mankind as they are, since we cannot have them as we wish." Another time he wrote to Governor William Livingston about his unrelenting challenges, and yet resolved, "I will not however despair." Washington's ability to cling to hope in the midst of crushing despair must have deeply impacted Hamilton and the rest of his staff.

* * *

How did the psalmist hold onto hope in the face of overwhelming despair? His awareness of self-talk is perhaps the most important factor. He doesn't passively allow discouraging thoughts to race through his mind, leading him deeper into despair. Instead of allowing his thoughts to define reality, he takes a step back and addresses himself. He talks to himself, instead of letting his thoughts talk to him.

Dr. Martyn Lloyd-Jones, in his book *Spiritual Depression*, points out the importance of this discipline in our lives: "We must talk to ourselves instead of allowing 'ourselves' to talk to us! . . . I suggest that the main trouble in this whole matter of spiritual depression in a sense is this, that we allow our self to talk to us instead of talking to our self." Lloyd-Jones then identifies this as the move made by the psalmist: "Instead of allowing this self to talk to him, he starts talking to himself. 'Why art thou downcast, O my soul?' he asks. His soul had been depressing him, crushing him. So he stands up and says: 'Self, listen for a moment, I will speak to you.'"

In seasons of despair, our self-talk can overwhelm us with negativity and hopelessness. I remember one season when I felt discouraged about ministry. I had just planted a new church, and nine months after the launch our growth plateaued. A few influential families decided to leave, and I could sense the loss of momentum. I began to doubt whether or not our community would survive, and shared my discouragement with a mentor. His first question cut straight to the heart of the matter, "How is your self-talk?" He knew me well. My negative self-talk compounded the problems in my leadership and self-confidence.

"Your church isn't going to make it."

"Everyone thinks you are a failure."

"It seems that God isn't interested in using you anymore. It's probably because you are such a disappointment to him."

Negative self-talk always leads us deeper into despair. We must grow in our mindfulness of how we talk to ourselves and eliminate negative self-talk. Psychologist Pamela E. Butler says, "We all talk to ourselves. What we say determines the direction and quality of our lives. Our self-talk can make the difference between happiness and despair, between self-confidence and self-doubt. Altering your self-talk may be the most important undertaking you will ever begin."

* * *

In seasons of despair we must learn to trust that God is working. The great Reformer, Martin Luther, struggled constantly with despair. His bouts with despair lasted for days, sometimes weeks. Some days he would be unable get out of bed, locking himself inside of his room. While initially despising his battles with despair, he came to understand his despair as an important aspect of the spiritual life. Without the experience of despair, Luther believed, one did not really know the truth of the spiritual life.

Mark Thompson writes, "Luther had no trouble in attributing [his despair] to the work of God in his life. [Despair is] God's instrument to strengthen faith, to cause us to abandon our self-reliance, and trust in Christ alone. In an important sense, we *must* despair of all else in order to wholeheartedly rely on Christ and what he has accomplished for us."

Luther came to believe that God used seasons of despair in his life to transform him, to teach him to more fully rely and trust in Christ. This contradicts our greatest fear when we face seasons of despair. We believe the presence of despair marks God's absence, his lack of concern, and even his lack of love. Luther believed the opposite. He saw seasons of despair as necessary seasons where God worked in important ways. When we learn to see this truth, we begin to see despair as a springboard to hope.

Recognizing this truth helps us to hope in the midst of despair. Luther writes of a spiritual "state in which hope despairs, and yet despair hopes as the same time." Luther did not see hope and despair as opposing, but rather concurrent realities. Despair looks around and sees the total absence of hope. Faith looks around and trusts that God is present and active, which always gives birth to hope.

* * *

Richard Rohr offers a beautiful phrase that captures this truth: Everything belongs. True spiritual maturity, Rohr suggests, is coming to a place where we fundamentally believe that God is a part of all things, that God works in all circumstances, that nothing resides beyond the purposes of God. God uses all the circumstances of our lives, even the ones that cause despair, to transform us. We just need to learn how to see this truth.

Rohr writes, "Spirituality is about seeing. . . . [O]nce you see, the rest follows. If we exist on a level where we can see how 'everything belongs,' we can trust the flow and trust the life, the life so large and deep and spacious that it even includes its opposite, death."

Holding onto hope that God works while we find ourselves in despair is the key. Rohr continues, "We can't leap over our grief work. Nor can we skip over our despair work. We have to feel it. That means that in our life we will have some blue days or dark days. Historical cultures saw grief as a time of incubation, transformation, and necessary hibernation. Yet this sacred space is the very space we avoid. When we avoid darkness, we avoid tension, spiritual creativity, and finally transformation."

The apostle Paul puts it this way: "And we know that in all things God works for the good of those who love him, who have been called according to his purpose." We know that in *all things*, not only the good things. Even the difficult things, the depressing things, the awful things. The things that sweep over us and try to drag us down into despair. In all things God is present, active, and working for our good.

* * *

Hamilton dominated the 2016 Tony Awards, winning eleven times. After winning the Tony for best original score, Miranda read for his acceptance speech a sonnet he had written earlier that day, June 12, 2016, after learning that patrons at a gay bar in Orlando, Florida, had been gunned down in the deadliest mass shooting by a single shooter in US history. Forty-nine people were killed, fifty-three more wounded. It was a senseless, tragic act of violence, the kind of event that makes us feel like the forces of darkness, chaos, and death will overwhelm this world. Yet that evening, Miranda called people to hope, reminding all of us that hope and love will never be defeated.

When we face despair, when the waves and breakers sweep over us, we must hold onto hope. We must remember that the love of God cannot ever be conquered—that in the end, light will overcome the darkness. We have to remember that even though it feels easier to give into despair, the path of the spiritual life is never the easy one.

Chapter Ten

Surrender

After Hamilton's political fall from grace, he could have let his ambition and pride dictate his next steps. It wouldn't have been out of character for Hamilton to pursue, with relentless passion and unwavering energy, a return to political power and influence. Surely part of him longed for a triumphant return to the government he helped build. Instead, Hamilton decided on a different path. He practiced, possibly for the first time in his life, the discipline of surrender.

During this season, Hamilton focused on his legal career and devoted much more time to his family. He purchased twenty-five acres of land north of the city, and began building an ambitious country home he would call the Grange. His motivation for this project stemmed from his growing desire to prioritize his family. "While all other passions decline in me, those of love and friendship gain new strength," he wrote to Eliza. "It will be more and more my endeavor to abstract myself from all pursuits which interfere with those of affection. 'Tis here only I can find true pleasure."

Tilar Mazzeo points out how Hamilton went to great lengths to demonstrate his commitment to Eliza and his family. "[Hamilton] surprises [Eliza] with the Grange, moves the family out of

New York City, and then goes to huge lengths to come home each night. He works all the way down at Wall Street, and then rides horseback, probably between eleven and fourteen miles, back home each night." Hamilton's actions communicate a real commitment to rebuild trust with Eliza.

At the Grange, gardening and landscaping became their shared passion. He wrote friends for agriculture advice, visited other gardens to obtain cuttings, and began designing and planting ambitious flower, vegetable, and fruit gardens. "He even communicated a political message through his gardening," writes Chernow. "Among the many shade trees that he dispersed around the grounds, he planted to the right of the front door a row of thirteen sweet gum trees meant to symbolize the union of the original thirteen states."

And yet even as he practiced this discipline of surrender, we see Hamilton struggling internally with his new reality. He wrote to a friend, "A garden, you know, is a very usual refuge of a disappointed politician."

* * *

Gardening offers a powerful image for surrender. To plant something in the ground requires one to relinquish the outcome. The elements exist beyond the gardener's control. The gardens Hamilton planted also suggest that he planned to put down roots outside of the city in this new season. He appears to have relinquished his former life of politics, surrendering to what this new season held for him and his family. Hamilton wrote letters to Eliza when she traveled, revealing a tender affection for their children. He enjoyed spending Sunday mornings in his garden, reading the Scriptures with them. After serving for more than twenty years at the very center of power and influence of this new country, Hamilton gracefully surrendered to a different path for his life.

George Washington might have mentored him in the art of graceful surrender. Washington's decision to step down from the presidency after his second term remains to this day one of the greatest acts of humility and surrender our country ever witnessed. Chernow writes, "Washington's decision to forgo a third term was momentous. He wasn't bound by term limits, and many Americans expected him to serve for life. He surrendered power in a world where leaders had always grabbed for more."

Washington's decision was his second remarkable act of surrender, the first being in 1783 after winning the Revolutionary War, when he peacefully stepped down as the general of the Continental Army. Washington wrote a document explaining his intentions to retire his position and move back to Mount Vernon. As a man of deep faith, Chernow writes, "the entire [document] had the pastoral tone of a spiritual father advising his flock." He ended his document with a clear call to following the example set by Jesus, "that he would most graciously be pleased to dispose us all to do Justice, to love mercy, and to demean ourselves with that Charity, humility, and pacific temper of mind, which were the characteristics of the Divine Author of our blessed religion; and without an humble imitation of whole example in these things, we can never hope to be a happy Nation." Washington embodied this "humble imitation," by surrendering in ways most men in power couldn't begin to fathom. When King George III heard about Washington's intention to step down, he responded, "If he does that, he will be the greatest man in the world."

Hamilton enjoyed a front row seat when Washington declined a third term as president, as Washington asked him to draft his farewell address. Hamilton's work was masterful. He gave "depth and scope and sterling expression to the overarching themes listed by Washington. . . . Their two voices blended admirably together. The result was a literary miracle," writes Chernow.

Miranda captures this blending of voices in the decision to surrender power brilliantly in his musical, as he does with so many historical details throughout the production. Hamilton begins reading the farewell address alone, but Washington joins in and they finish the text reading together in a unified voice. Hamilton's ability to gracefully surrender his public ambitions when his turn came had to have been partially influenced by this historic moment.

In our lives, surrendering is so difficult, and yet central to our call as followers of Jesus. God commands us to be a people who surrender our will to him. Psalm 37:7 calls us to "Surrender yourself to the Lord, and wait patiently for him." Living this out proves elusive.

* * *

Ann Voskamp shares a story about surrender in her book *One Thousand Gifts*. Her brother-in-law, John, had a son named

Austin, who at only four months old died of a genetic disease. A year and a half later, a second son was born, named Dietrich. Voskamp writes that Dietrich was "born to hopes and prayers."

I can imagine this family begging God for this second son to be born healthy, praying that he would be spared this disease. Hoping that this son would have the chance to grow up, to learn how to ride a bike, that John might teach him how to throw a baseball. That this son might even someday have a family of his own. But their prayers went unanswered. Dietrich was born into this world with the same terminal diagnosis as his brother, and died five months after his birth. This family had buried two sons in less than two years.

In the hospital, Voskamp recounted the conversation she had with John after Dietrich died. John's response shocked me: "We're just blessed," he said. "Up until today Dietrich's had no pain. We have good memories of a happy Christmas. That's more than we had with Austin. Tiffany's got lots and lots of pictures. And we had five months with him."

Voskamp's response was quite different, and much more familiar to me. She writes, "I grab him by the shoulders and I look straight into those eyes, brimming. And in this scratchy, half whisper, these ragged words choke—*wail*. 'If it were up to me . . .' and the words pound, desperate and hard, 'I'd write this story differently.'"

I can relate to her response in this story: anger, confusion, defiance. This is not how this story should go! Who in the hell is in charge around here anyway? But John surrenders, somehow seeing God's will in this. He submits to his son's death—with grief, with a crushed spirit, with dashed hopes. Yet he neverthe-less submits. In doing so, he practices one of the most impor-tant disciplines in our lives with God.

Teresa of Avila, a master of the interior spiritual life writes, "Whoever makes a habit of prayer should think only of doing everything to conform his will to God's. Be assured that in this conformity consists the highest perfection we can attain, and those who practice it with the greatest care will be favored by God's greatest gift and will make the quickest progress in the interior life. Do not imagine there are other secrets. All our good consists in this."

* * *

Recognizing how little control we have in the first place helps us in the difficult task of surrendering. So much of what happens in our lives is simply out of our hands. Washington explains this truth to Hamilton as the war comes to an end. He sings about how little control we have over life, death, and the legacy that we leave behind. This idea captures one of the central truths of Miranda's musical. Miranda observes, "Once I wrote this passage, I knew it would be the key to the whole musical. . . . We strut and fret our hour upon the stage, and how that reverberates is entirely out of our control."

* * *

The garden of Gethsemane offers one of the most powerful stories of surrender in the Scriptures. New Testament scholar Joel Green considers Gethsemane "the watershed [moment] in the passion narrative." In this moment, Jesus decides whether he will surrender to the will of God, no matter the cost. We all know how the story ends, but we often underestimate how deeply Jesus struggled to surrender to his Father. We have a hard time imagining how close Jesus came to saying no to God's will.

The Gospel of Mark tells us that Jesus went to Gethsemane with his disciples to pray. He asked Peter, James, and John, his three closest friends, to share his agony. He shared with them that his soul was overwhelmed with sorrow to the point of death. He asked them to sit and keep watch while he prayed.

Mark reads, "Going a little father, he fell to the ground and prayed that if possible the hour might pass from him. 'Abba, Father,' he said, 'everything is possible for you. Take this cup from me. Yet not what I will, but what you will.'"

Jesus begs God, his Father, for another way. He shudders at the horrors of what lies before him. Betrayal. Beating. Flogging. Humiliation. Crucifixion. He longs with everything inside of him for another way, tormented by what lies ahead of him. He is a man about to come unhinged.

The name Gethsemane, a Hebrew word meaning "oil press" or "the place where olive oil is pressed," provides insight into Jesus' anguish. The garden of Gethsemane, a small olive grove located on the Mount of Olives, overlooked Jerusalem. The value in the olives resided in the oil that had to be pressed out of them, a process that Hebrew scholar Ray Vander Laan describes. First, ripe olives would be placed into a stone basin where a large millstone rolled over the olives, crushing them into pulp. Next, heavy stone slabs were lowered onto the crushed olives, slabs whose weight pressed the olive oil out of the pulp. The oil would run down into a pit, to be collected and sold.

This process offers a powerful image for how Jesus felt that night. His calling had become a millstone, rolling over him, crushing him into a pulp. Heavy slabs of fear lowered onto him, pressing the life out of him. The Gospel of Luke tells us that Jesus experienced such anguish that his sweat became like drops of blood, a medical phenomenon that doctors acknowledge as a physical response to enormous stress and pressure. The pressure Jesus felt literally squeezed the very life blood out of him. It would soon flow much more freely. God asked Jesus to surrender to his will, to the cross, and this reality crushed him.

N. T. Wright describes Jesus' torment: "Jesus was like a man walking in a nightmare. He could see, as though it was before his very eyes, the cup. . . . The cup of God's wrath. He didn't want to drink it. He badly didn't want to. Jesus at this point was no hero-figure, marching boldly towards his oncoming fate. . . . He was a man, as we might say, in melt-down mode. He had looked into the darkness and seen the grinning faces of all the demons in the world looking back at him. And he begged and begged his father not to bring him to the point of going through with it. . . . And the answer was No."

The call to surrender our will to God's can feel at times like a crushing weight. When God says no, when he asks us to surrender, we echo Jesus' prayer: "Father God, all things are possible. Take this cup from me!" We pray this prayer when life doesn't turn out the way we hoped. We never imagined ourselves failing in our career, as a single parent, or addicted to alcohol or pornography. We beg God, "All things are possible for you! Heal me Lord. Open this door. Help me find a spouse or a job. Give me a different path, save me from this suffering!" And yet sometimes, like that night in the garden with Jesus, God says no.

Jesus finishes his prayer with an act of surrender, "Yet not what I will, but what you will." Jesus proves his fidelity to God by laying down what he wants and obeying God. Even though doing so costs him everything, even his very life.

* * *

Hamilton knew this longing for God to save him from suffering, to provide another way. After his son Philip had been shot in his duel with Eacker, Hamilton and Eliza rushed to the house where he had been taken. Dr. David Hosack, at the house caring for Philip, relates Hamilton's response. "[Hamilton] instantly turned from the bed and, taking me by the hand, which he grasped with all the agony of grief, he exclaimed in a tone and manner than can never be effaced from my memory, 'Doctor, I despair.'"

Both Alexander and Eliza stayed by Philip's bed throughout the agonizing night. It is not difficult to imagine them begging God, like Jesus at Gethsemane, for another way. "All things are possible for you God! Take this cup from us! Please don't let our son's life end this way."

Their prayers went unanswered, as Philip died at five in the morning. A few months later, Hamilton repeated a version of Jesus' surrender in the garden. In one letter, he wrote, "It was the will of heaven and he is now out of the reach of the seductions and calamities of a world full of folly, full of vice, full of danger. . . . I firmly trust also that he has safely reached the haven of eternal repose and felicity."

* * *

Jesus found the strength to surrender to God's will because he trusted God. Jesus articulates this trust in the beginning of his prayer in the garden: "Abba, Father." *Abba* is an intimate word in Hebrew, what a young child would call his father. Jesus, facing the most difficult decision of his time on this earth, begins his prayer by addressing his father as daddy. They share an intimate, trusting relationship.

Jesus trusted God, not only in this moment, but throughout his life, in every moment, every situation, every decision he faced. Proverbs 3 calls us to this same trust: "Trust in the Lord with all your heart and lean not on your own understanding; in all your ways submit to him, and he will make your paths straight."

When we fail to surrender to God's will, it betrays a lack of trust. Every time we say no to God's will, we essentially say to him: I do not trust you. I do not trust you to fulfill my needs, to satisfy my deepest desires. I do not trust that you have my best interests at heart and that you know what is best for me.

When God calls us to surrender, it can feel counterintuitive. In the moment it can feel like a crushing burden, even like death, like we are giving up on the best path for our lives. But the decision to trust, to surrender to God's will, always leads us into our best life, into the eternal life now.

Trust surrenders, even when we don't fully understand. Our perspective is so limited, but God can see the entire arc of our stories. John, the father who lost his two boys, reminds us of this truth: "Well, even with our boys . . . I don't know why that all happened. . . . But do I have to. . . ? Maybe you don't want to change the story, because you don't know what a different ending holds. . . . Maybe . . . I guess . . . it's accepting there are things we simply don't understand. But he does." Voskamp writes, "There is a reason I am not writing the story and God is. He knows how it all works out, where it all leads, what it all means. I *don't*."

Throughout Jesus' life, he practiced the habit of surrendering to God in the small, daily decisions, "For I have come down from heaven not to do my will but to do the will of him who sent me." This habit of surrendering in every decision, no matter how small, created a pattern for Jesus to follow when he had to surrender in this enormous decision.

Saint Claude de la Colombiere writes in his book, *Trustful Surrender to Divine Providence*, about the importance of the "frequent practice of the virtue of submission. But as the opportunities for practicing it in a big way come rather seldom, we must take advantage of the small ones which occur daily, and which will soon put us in a position to face the greater trials with equanimity when the time comes."

* * *

A good friend of mine, Genny, practiced the habit of surrender. She loved God and served him with her life, following him into a number of different ministry callings. She continually sought out God's will in her life. She established a habit of surrendering to God in her daily, sometimes seemingly insignificant, decisions. The habit of surrender had already been established when Genny was diagnosed with an aggressive form of breast cancer at the age of thirty-three.

The doctors performed a double mastectomy, and she underwent six rounds of intensive chemotherapy. An intimate part of her was cut from her body, she lost her hair, and suffered significant side effects from the chemo. She lived a nightmare for six grueling months. Pressures, stress, and anxieties pressed down hard on her and her family. Remarkably, Genny suffered through this battle against cancer with an extraordinary posture of surrender.

She received her diagnosis during the season of Lent. After the diagnosis, the Lord immediately brought to her mind the story of the garden of Gethsemane. "I connected, during this season, in a different way with the humanity of Jesus," she recounted. "Before cancer, I really didn't understand his humanity. When the doctors explained my treatment plan, I entered a season of waiting for it all to begin. I really related to Jesus, that evening in the garden, when he prayed, 'I don't want to do this, take this away. I don't want to suffer.'"

A few years before Genny received her diagnosis, the Lord challenged her with a phrase: are you going to be willing or willful? "I'm a really willful person," she said. "Strong, confident, maybe a little bossy. I began practicing that phrase of being either willful or willing in small ways. In how much I used my phone. In how much I spent on coffee. I practiced being willing to what the Lord asked me to do."

When cancer crashed down onto her life, she practiced that same discipline, surrendering to the Lord by being willing instead of willful. She had already developed the habit. She surrendered so much: the loss of her breasts, her hair, her energy, and strength. She surrendered control over her life. "I was at the mercy of the doctors' wisdom and medicine to live. It was a very vulnerable place for me to be at the age of thirty-three." Genny's posture of surrender led her, throughout her battle, to a place of trust, peace, and acceptance. She powerfully witnessed to everyone around her the truth that surrender leads us into life.

Every time we choose to surrender our will to God's, we find our best life, our greatest good. Although it might seem counterintuitive, although it might feel like death, this path leads us into the eternal life now. Jesus chose this path in the garden, and calls us to embody the courage, strength, and faith required to follow where he leads.

* * *

Hamilton's final act of surrender occurred during his duel with Aaron Burr. Leading up to the duel, Hamilton resolved to employ the same strategy he advised for his son: He would intentionally fire into the air. He wrote, "I have resolved, if our interview is conducted in the usual manner, and it pleases God to give me the opportunity, to *reserve* and *throw away* my first fire, and I have thoughts even of reserving my second fire—and thus giving a double opportunity to Col. Burr to pause and reflect." He told Nathaniel Pendleton, who served as his second for the duel, "It is the effect of a religious scruple and does not admit of reasoning." He wrote to Eliza, "But you had rather I should die innocent than live guilty."

Great irony exists in the fact that Hamilton, who lived his life always taking the initiative, refused to raise his pistol in his duel with Burr. He surrendered the outcome—a decision that tragically would cost him his life. Every act of surrender, in ways big and small, requires the same dying to self in us.

Chapter Eleven

Death

Hamilton, like all who lived in the late 1700s, was all too familiar with the unrelenting force of death. War, a lack of medical understanding, and a high infant mortality rate all contributed to an average life expectancy of only thirty-six years. In many towns, church bells would ring out to honor the deceased. During this era, some towns outlawed this ringing of the bells because of how frequently it occurred. Communities grew weary of constantly hearing the church bells announce yet another death in their midst.

We have already seen how death ravished Hamilton's family in his early years. By the age of fourteen, death had stolen away almost every family member that Hamilton had known. Throughout the Revolutionary War, many of Hamilton's friends, including his closest friend John Laurens, sacrificed their lives in the fight for freedom.

The death of his beloved son Philip ushered both Eliza and Alexander into intense pain and suffering, which Hamilton never fully recovered from. One of Hamilton's friends described him as having a "face [that had been] strongly stamped with grief," a truth that a portrait of Hamilton during his later years visibly captured. Sorrow and grief completely overwhelmed Hamilton's life. Such is the devastating power and force of death.

* * *

My uncle Roger died when he was in his mid-thirties. An alcoholic, he drank until his liver failed. One evening, he drank until he passed out, and a friend rushed him to the hospital where his doctors miraculously saved his life. They told him if he continued to drink, he would die. But he couldn't stop. He kept drinking, and died a few months later.

I'll never forget a scene from his funeral. My grandfather sat at the end of the front pew with the rest of our family. I looked at him and witnessed on his face an intensity of grief and sorrow I had never seen before. His face, like Hamilton's portrait, strongly stamped with grief. Tears streamed down his cheeks as he grappled with the finality of burying his son.

Years later, I had the opportunity to spend time with my grandfather's best friend, Frank. Roger came up at one point during our conversation, and Frank told me that after Roger died, my grandfather was never the same. Something shifted inside of him that forever altered his life. Such is the power of death.

* * *

Facing death creates a powerful fear in all of us. In his Pulitzer Prize-winning book *The Denial of Death*, author Ernest Becker suggests that the fear of death drives much of our behavior. He writes, "Of all things that move man, one of the principal ones is his terror of death. . . . The fear of death is natural and is present in everyone . . . it is the basic fear that influences all others, a fear from which no one is immune, no matter how disguised it may be."

This fear includes not only the physical death we will someday face, but the thousands of deaths we suffer in our day-to-day lives. Author Michael Pasquarello III writes that we experience "countless unnoticed, forgotten, and smaller forms of loss, death, and the diminishment of life. Relationships grow cold, sour, and end; hurt and disappointment come from those we love; life seems to be unjust or senseless; failure and discouragement accompany our noblest intentions. . . . We know all too well the reality of tears, pain, sadness, darkness, suffering, and death."

The *Hamilton* cast came face to face with this brutal reality when Oskar Eustis, who opened the show at the Public Theatre and continued as an important member on Miranda's team, lost his sixteen-year-old son Jack. The loss devastated the *Hamilton* community. Miranda sent an email to Eustis after hearing of his loss, sharing words of comfort. He also sent them a demo recording of the song "It's Quiet Uptown," his song about the Hamiltons losing their son. Miranda remembered thinking, "There is nothing you can say, and yet, I had a song about this." Miranda wrote to the Eustises, "If art can help us grieve, can help us mourn, then lean on it." Eustis later said, "Every line of 'Quiet Uptown' feels like it's exactly correct to my experience. It was the only music [my wife and I] listened to for a long time, and we listened to it every day, and it became a key thing for the two of us."

* * *

Jerry Sittser shares his story of unimaginable pain, loss, and death in his book *A Grace Disguised*. One night, while driving home with his family on an isolated, two-lane highway, a car approached from the opposite direction. The other driver was drunk and swerved into his lane, colliding head-on with the Sittsers' family minivan. Sittser's daughter, wife, and mother all died in the crash. He and his three other children survived.

Sittser writes, "In the hours that followed the accident, the initial shock gave way to an unspeakable agony. I felt dizzy with grief's vertigo, cut off from family and friends, tormented by the loss, nauseous from the pain. . . . I could not stop crying. I could not silence the deafening noise of crunching metal, screaming sirens, and wailing children. I could not rid my eyes of the vision of violence, of shattering glass and shattered bodies. All I wanted was to be dead."

The morning of the funeral he wanted to view all three bodies before the service. "I visited the funeral home and stared in disbelief at three open coffins before me. At that moment I felt myself slipping into a black hole of dread and oblivion. I was afloat in space, utterly alone among billions of nameless, distant stars. . . . Never have I experienced such anguish and emptiness."

When I hear a story like this, my insides churn. Sittser's story confronts my greatest fear. Can you imagine death assaulting your life like this, dramatically altering your life in an instant? Living with this kind of pain and loss?

Sittser writes, "Loss reminds us that we do not have the final word. Death does, whether it be the death of a spouse, a friendship, a marriage, a job, or our health. In the end, death conquers all."

* * *

This sentiment captures how Hamilton's family and friends felt after his death. Only thirty-six hours prior, Hamilton had rowed across the Hudson River to meet Burr at Weehawken for their duel—tragically, at the same spot that his son had been shot and killed. The duel stemmed from years of political clashes between the two men, what Ellis calls "a culmination of long-standing personal animosity and political disagreement that emerged naturally, in retrospect, almost inevitably, out of the supercharged political culture of the early republic."

After numerous disagreements and insults, Burr's patience wore out. He felt so personally dishonored by Hamilton that he wrote to him and demanded an apology. Hamilton could have apologized and ended the conflict right then. Instead, he replied in a way that seemed to intentionally spur Burr on. The conflict spiraled out of control, and Burr challenged Hamilton to a duel, which Hamilton accepted.

On the dueling field, Hamilton used the same strategy he advised his son Phillip to take: He would intentionally fire into the air. Burr, however, had different plans. He shot Hamilton in the side, delivering a wound that would end with Hamilton's death. Hamilton was quickly taken back to a friend's home, where for two days his family and friends endured a scene of unbearable grief. Gouverneur Morris, a Founding Father from New York, described the scene: "his wife almost frantic with grief, his children in tears, every person present deeply afflicted, the whole city agitated, every countenance dejected."

Chernow describes one particularly heartbreaking scene. Eliza, realizing the nearness of her husband's death, gathered up their seven children. She lifted up their two-year-old son, Philip, to give one final kiss. Then, the children stood at the foot of the bed Hamilton lay in to say their last goodbyes. Hamilton was so overcome by grief that "he opened his eyes, gave them one look, and closed them again until they were taken away," recounted Dr. Hosack, the physician present at Hamilton's death. Hamilton, overcome by the reality of death, couldn't even bear to look at his children. Such is the power of death. It seems to conquer all.

* * *

When we look at the death of Jesus, a different possibility emerges. Jesus' life and ministry threatened the Jewish religious elite and the structures that kept them in power. Jesus welcomed sinners, confronted religious leaders, judged what the Jewish religious system had become, and even claimed he was the Son of God. The Jewish leaders collaborated with the Roman authorities to remove this threat.

Jesus was arrested, sentenced at a mock trial, beaten, spit upon, flogged, and crucified. After Roman soldiers nailed him to the cross, darkness covered the land from noon until three in the afternoon. Jesus cried out, "My God, my God, why have you forsaken me?" Then, he gave up his spirit and died.

After Jesus died, all of his disciples, followers, and even his enemies knew this moment marked the end of the story. The next verse in the Gospels after Jesus' death might as well have read "The End." Everyone present that day believed the end had come for Jesus.

Jesus' followers had placed their hopes and dreams in him. They believed he was the Messiah, the one their people had longed for. They had seen him perform miracles, even raise people from the dead. They believed he would be the one to finally set Israel free. But now, the story came to a painful and abrupt stop, and his followers felt totally, utterly, completely crushed. His enemies felt thankful to be rid of this threat. Both sides believed, and knew, that death had the final word.

But the next verse in the Gospel of Matthew does not read "the end." Verse 51 begins with "At that moment." An interesting phrase in Greek, it could be translated literally as "and, look," or "behold." This Greek phrase suggests that something important is about to happen.

My Bible language dictionary says that this phrase is a marker of strong emphasis, involving surprise and unexpectedness. It also serves as a prompter of attention, a phrase that emphasizes the following statement. This phrase says, in essence, "Look. Listen. *Pay attention!*"

My youngest son Levi, a five-year-old, wants my full attention all of the time. His insistence on my attention can feel, at times, a bit exhausting. He constantly says, "Daddy, look! Daddy, look! Look how fast I can run! Look how high I can jump! Look how much mud I can fit into your shoes!" Levi doesn't want me to miss what is about to happen next.

When Matthew writes the words "at that moment," right after Jesus dies, he says to all of us, "Behold! Look! Listen! Pay attention! Daddy, look! You don't want to miss what happens next!"

* * *

What happens next refutes our idea that death has the final word. The curtain of the temple is torn in two, from top to bottom. This curtain separated the holy of holies, the place where the Jewish people believed God's very presence dwelt, from the rest of the temple. Now the curtain was torn in two, from the top to the bottom, suggesting God himself caused this tearing. Because of the death of Jesus, all people now had direct access to God. No curtain necessary.

Next, the earth shook and the rocks split. This earthquake signified God's presence in this awful event. In the Old Testament, a prophecy talks about mountains quaking and the earth trembling at the presence of God. God affirms in the earthquake that this story will continue, that the end has not arrived. He announces that something profound has taken place in this moment, a decisive event that no one can comprehend quite yet.

Then, the bodies of many holy people who had died were raised to life, marking the inauguration of the resurrection life. The death of Jesus somehow overcomes and defeats the power of death. Jesus death marks not the end, but the beginning. And we haven't even gotten to the bodily resurrection of Jesus yet!

Death, Matthew communicates to us, will not have the final word.

* * *

We see this truth in the words Jesus cries out on the cross, "My God, My God, why have you forsaken me?" This cry articulates Jesus' experience of total desperation, his feeling of utter forsakenness by his Father. At the same time, however, Jesus' cry articulates a deeper truth.

With this cry, Jesus quotes Psalm 22, written by King David. David also cried out to God, during his experience of forsakenness. David writes, "My God, my God, why have you forsaken me? Why are you so far from saving me, so far from my cries of anguish? My God, I cry out by day, but you do not answer, by night, but I find no rest." He describes how death surrounds and presses in on him. "Many bulls surround me. . . . Roaring lions that tear their prey open their mouths wide against me. . . . Dogs surround me, a pack of villains encircle me."

David feels forsaken by God, his very life threatened, while God seems to do nothing. David questions why God abandons him, instead of rescuing him. Jesus articulates these same struggles when he quotes David's psalm on the cross.

In the second half of the psalm, the tone shifts. David offers thanksgiving and praise to God because of God's vindication. God has heard his prayer, proved himself faithful to David, making Psalm 22 an ultimate prayer of vindication: "I will declare your name to my people; in the assembly I will praise you. You who fear the LORD, praise him! All you descendants of Jacob, honor him! Revere him, all you descendants of Israel! For he has not despised or scorned the suffering of the afflicted one; he has not hidden his face from him but has listened to his cry for help."

This psalm begins in doubt and darkness, with David feeling forsaken by God. But it ends in faith and praise, with God vindicating David. When Jesus quotes this psalm on the cross, on one hand, he is honestly speaking about his current desperation. He feels utterly forsaken by God, and articulates the incredible sadness and pain we feel when we come face to face with death and loss. At the same time, however, Jesus quotes Psalm 22 as a prayer of vindication. He declares that even in his death, God will somehow vindicate him. Death, Jesus proclaims, will not have the final word.

* * *

Paul explains the hope of resurrection, in a passage from 1 Corinthians 15: "At the same moment and in the same way, we'll all be changed. In the resurrection scheme of things, this has to happen: everything perishable taken off the shelves and replaced by the imperishable, this mortal replaced by the immortal. Then the saying will come true: Death swallowed up by triumphant Life! Who got the last word, oh, Death? Oh, Death, who's afraid of you now?"

Because of the death and resurrection of Jesus, Paul asserts, we live with faith that death will not have the final word. We see this truth captured in the song "The World Was Wide Enough." This scene portrays the duel between Burr and Hamilton. After Burr pulls the trigger on his pistol, time freezes, and Hamilton offers a brilliant soliloquy about his life and death. This song provides the only moment of the show where Hamilton speaks without music. During his speech, he looks up and catches a glimpse of heaven, a glimpse of the other side. As the bullet approaches him, Hamilton enters into a thin place. He experiences a transcendent moment. He sees Laurens, his son Philip, his mother, and Washington all looking down at him from heaven. Death, Hamilton reminds us, does not have the final word. Another life awaits us on the other side.

We also see this truth in Hamilton's response to his impending death. The scene at his deathbed offers clear evidence of his faith in God and belief that death does not have the final word. Chernow writes, "Hamilton was preoccupied with spiritual matters in a way that eliminates all doubt about the sincerity of his late-flowering religious interests."

Hamilton longed to receive his last rites, and asked his friend and clergyman, the Reverend John M. Mason, to administer them to him. Chernow recounts the conversation between the two men, "Mason tried to console Hamilton by saying that all men had sinned and were equal in the Lord's sight. 'I perceive it to be so,' Hamilton said. 'I am a sinner. I look to His mercy. . . .' As Mason told how Christ's blood would wash away his sins, Hamilton grasped his hand, rolled his eyes heavenward, and exclaimed with fervor, 'I have a tender reliance on the mercy of the Almighty, through the merits of the Lord Jesus Christ.'" At the end of Hamilton's life, he truly did catch a glimpse of the other side.

* * *

The truth of the resurrection impacts the way we live today, the choices we make, and where we invest our lives. Jesus' resurrection gives us faith to press on in the midst of despair, courage to move forward in the face of failure, hope in the midst of the most hopeless circumstances.

Kate Bowler was diagnosed with stage four cancer at the age of thirty-five. The diagnosis, as you can imagine, crushed her and her family. She struggled to move forward. Yet somehow, she continued to press on into life. She writes,

> Cancer has kicked down the walls of my life. . . . But cancer has also ushered in new ways of being alive. . . . [E]verything feels as if it is painted in bright colors. In my vulnerability, I am seeing my world without the Instagrammed filter of breezy certainties and perfectible moments. I can't help noticing the brittleness of the walls that keep most people fed, sheltered and whole. I find myself returning to the same thoughts again and again: *Life is so beautiful. Life is so hard.*

Bowler lives in the tension between death and resurrection, the tension in Psalm 22, the tension Jesus experiences on the cross. Death is a crushing and devastating reality and, at times, feels like it will have the final word. We all experience moments where death, chaos, and darkness overwhelm our lives. Life is so hard.

And yet, in the face of that death, we affirm the goodness of life, the hope of resurrection. We believe, even when it seems naïve or foolish, that death does not have the final word. We live with courage, hope, and faith, in the face of the relentless onslaught of death in our lives. We look for moments that remind that life is so beautiful.

* * *

Jerry Sittser found the grace of God in the midst of death, a grace that enabled him to move forward and live his life. He writes,

> Gifts of grace come to all of us. But we must be ready to see and willing to receive these gifts. It will require a kind of sacrifice, the sacrifice of believing that, however painful our losses, life can still be good—good in a different way than before, but nevertheless good. . . . I will always want the ones I lost back again. I long for them with all my soul. But I still celebrate the life I have found because they are gone. I have lost, but I have also gained. I lost the world I loved, but I gained a deeper awareness of grace.

Christ's death and resurrection make this grace possible. Sittser writes, "Jesus had been killed, had somehow absorbed sin, evil, and death into himself, and had been raised from the grave. The resurrection was his vindication. Death does not have the final word; life does."

* * *

Throughout the final hours of Hamilton's life, as he lay dying in his friend's bed, he encouraged Eliza with a phrase he hoped would help her through her grief. He repeated to his wife, again and again, the words, "Remember, my Eliza, you are a Christian." He believed this central truth would enable her to regain a sense of hope in the midst of crushing loss.

In our own struggle facing death, both physical death and the thousands of deaths we face in our everyday lives, Hamilton's phrase offers us remarkable wisdom and perspective. It reminds us that we believe in something more powerful than death.

Remember, you are a Christian.

Remember, you believe that death will not have the final word. Remember, you believe in the life, death, and resurrection of Jesus—a resurrection we will all experience one day. Remember, you believe that this world is temporary, that death is not the end but the beginning of life eternal. Remember, you believe that one day, God will destroy death once and for all and create a new heaven and a new earth. He will wipe every tear from our eyes, and there will be no more death or mourning or crying or pain. Remember, you believe that the old order of things will pass away, and that Jesus will make all things new.

Remember, you are a Christian. That means death can never have the final word. Life does.

Chapter Twelve

Redemption

The musical *Hamilton* resonates with me more than any piece of art I have ever experienced, primarily because it teems with the most important themes of my life. Engaging these themes of grace, shame, forgiveness, and surrender through Hamilton's story encourages, inspires, and transforms me. But above all other themes, Hamilton's story resonates with me because, ultimately, it tells a story that I desperately need to experience: it tells a story of redemption.

When I take an honest assessment of my life, I see brokenness everywhere. I live with mixed motives, impure thoughts, and selfish actions. When I look at the world around me, more so today than ever, it appears to be constantly assaulted by the forces of brokenness. Death, terrorism, poverty, and divisiveness seem to win the day. My own life, and the world that we all live in, both share an acute desperation for redemption.

Hamilton moves people because it reminds us of this possibility. Interestingly, Hamilton is not the driving force behind this redemption, but rather his loving, faithful, and determined wife, Eliza. She takes the brokenness from his life and makes it beautiful.

The greatest source of pain and brokenness in Hamilton's life originated from his status as an orphan, a reality that haunted him throughout his life. Hamilton, like most orphans, surely grew up feeling abandoned, unwanted, and unloved, hounded by loneliness and inadequacy.

I read an article written by an orphan named David, who experienced a deep sense of abandonment and rejection, feelings he struggled with into his late fifties. Another girl whose parents died wrote that orphans grow up rarely feeling special or loved. They wear secondhand clothes, play with used toys, and rarely celebrate their birthdays. Many orphans don't even know the date of their birthday.

I can imagine heartbreaking conversations where Hamilton shared his pain and suffering from being an orphan with Eliza. I can also imagine Eliza, as any loving spouse would, feeling a deep sense of empathy about Hamilton's struggles as an orphan. Hamilton's brokenness must have become her brokenness, as she carried his burden with her husband. After Hamilton's death, and after she healed from her grief, Eliza took that hurt, suffering, and brokenness, and gave everything she could to redeem it, to make it new.

* * *

The poet R. M. Drake writes about humanity's brokenness on Instagram, with more than one million followers. His words resonate because he acknowledges the reality of our brokenness, while also offering hope that it can somehow be made beautiful, be made new. Drake writes, "To be human is to be broken, and broken is its own kind of beautiful."

Or this: "And she always had a way with her brokenness. She would take her pieces and make them beautiful." Drake articulates the longing deep inside each of us, the longing that our brokenness might somehow be made new.

This hope for redemption forms a powerful and central theme throughout the Scriptures, a hope captured in a scene from Mel Gibson's *Passion of the Christ*. Jesus carries his cross through Jerusalem, on his way to the site of his crucifixion. The Roman soldiers have beaten, bloodied, and broken his body, almost beyond recognition. As he stumbles through the streets of Jerusalem, Roman soldiers whip him, Jewish leaders mock him, the brokenness of humanity appears to consume him. Eventually, Jesus' strength fails him under the weight of the cross he carries, and he collapses to the ground.

A few feet away, his mother Mary watches him fall to the ground, paralyzed by terror and fear. She turns her face away, unable to observe this gruesome scene play out.

As she turns away, a memory of Jesus as a little boy, maybe three years old, flashes into her mind. He smiles and plays in a courtyard, then stumbles to the ground, hurting himself. Mary rushes over to him, picks him up in her arms, and comforts him. "I am here," she says.

Immediately after that memory, she springs to her feet and rushes to her son again, now a grown man, his blood spilling onto the ground. She fights her way through the crowd, past the

Roman soldiers, and falls to the ground where Jesus lies. "I am here," she cries out to him.

Jesus, beaten, bloodied, broken, on his way to his crucifixion and death, touches her face and inexplicably says to her, "See Mother, I make all things new." He wraps his arms around his cross, wills himself up from the ground, and presses on to his crucifixion.

As Jesus stumbles away, a look of bewilderment crosses Mary's face. All she can see in this moment is violence, brokenness, and death. She struggles to comprehend how this brokenness can be made new. It requires extraordinary faith to believe in redemption when darkness and death press in all around us.

After Alexander died, grief overwhelmed Eliza. Chernow writes, "For Eliza Hamilton, the collapse of her world was total, overwhelming, and remorseless. Within three years, she had had to cope with four close deaths: her eldest son, her sister Peggy, her mother, and her husband, not to mention the mental breakdown of her eldest daughter." Chernow shares that immediately after the death of Hamilton, Eliza invited Gouverneur Morris, a close family friend, into the room, then "burst into tears, told him he was the best friend her husband had, begged him to join her in prayers for her own death, and then to be a father for her children."

Eliza, in this moment, found herself completely overwhelmed by brokenness and death. Like Mary, she couldn't even begin to imagine redemption. But in time, God would give her faith to see the possibility of redemption out of the brokenness. Eventually, she would take Hamilton's pieces and make them beautiful.

* * *

The line Jesus declares to his mother, "See, I make all things new," actually comes from the Book of Revelation, where the resurrected Jesus sits upon his throne. Gibson reimagines Jesus speaking these words in a conversation with his mother, right in the middle of his suffering, passion, and death. Gibson makes a brilliant theological move in this reimagining, placing Jesus on his throne in the midst of his passion.

The full passage reads, "Then I saw 'a new heaven and a new earth,' for the first heaven and the first earth had passed away, and there was no longer any sea. I saw the Holy City, the new Jerusalem coming down out of heaven from God. . . . He who was seated on the throne said, 'I am making everything new!'"

The very last book of the Bible, the very end of the story, returns to themes established in the beginning. In the creation story in Genesis, God creates the heavens and the earth. In Revelation, God creates a new heaven and a new earth. In Genesis, the story begins with chaos, represented by the waters, a powerful image for the forces of chaos, destruction, and death throughout the Scriptures. In Revelation 21, however, the sea no longer exists. The forces of evil and chaos have finally, once and for all, been defeated by God. The author of Revelation offers a vision of the new creation. Jesus, seated on the throne, makes this clear, declaring, "I am making all things new."

Eugene Peterson observes, "The biblical story began, quite logically, with a beginning. Now it draws to an end, not quite so logically, also with a beginning. The sin-ruined creation of Genesis is restored in the sacrifice-renewed creation of Revelation." Everything broken in all of creation, God promises to make new.

* * *

The characters in Jesus' resurrection narrative personally experience this glorious redemption. Mary Magdalene, one of Jesus' followers, walks to his tomb the morning after his burial. She arrives at his tomb and finds it empty. Grief erupts out of her heart; John's narrative states that Mary cried or wept four different times. But then Jesus appears to her in his resurrected body, she falls at his feet, and in an instant, her grief transforms into joy. Mary is made new.

Later that evening, the disciples huddle together behind locked doors, terrified that they will soon share Jesus' fate. Out of nowhere, Jesus stands among them and gives them his peace. "Peace be with you! As the Father has sent me, I am sending you." Their all-consuming fear transforms into peace. The disciples are made new.

Thomas, absent when Jesus appeared to the other disciples, remains skeptical. The disciples tell him they have seen the resurrected Lord, but he cannot dare to believe. "Unless I see the nail marks in his hands and put my finger where the nails were, and put my hand into his side, I will not believe," he stubbornly declares. Thomas doubts because he feels too much pain; it will hurt too badly to face disappointment again. He closes himself off to the possibility of hope. Jesus appears to him, meets him in his doubt, and offers the very conditions that Thomas needed to believe, "Put your finger here; see my hands. Reach out your hand and put it into my side. Stop doubting and believe." Thomas moves from doubt to faith. He is made new.

Peter had failed Jesus, denied that he knew him three times, just as Jesus predicted. Now Peter must live with that devastating failure for the rest of his life. Crushed with guilt, shame, and remorse, Peter hates what he has done, and maybe even hates himself. In the midst of Peter's failure, Jesus appears to Peter and makes his brokenness beautiful, asking him three times if he loves him. Each question provides an opportunity to redeem the failure of his three denials. Peter moves from failure to forgiveness. Peter is made new.

The story of Jesus' resurrection leads to actual, tangible redemption for his disciples; their brokenness is made new. The resurrection of Jesus announces the birth of the new creation, born out of brokenness, chaos, and death. What God did for Jesus in the resurrection, and his disciples in the Easter story, God will do for all of us today. He calls us to move from grief to joy, from fear to peace, from doubt to faith, from failure to forgiveness. God intends to bring redemption out of our brokenness, he promises to make all of us new, and he calls us to believe in that possibility.

* * *

Eliza slowly recovered from her grief, finding solace in her faith in God. "Suffering from the 'irreparable loss of a most amiable and affectionate husband,' she prayed for 'the mercies of the divine being in whose dispensations' all Christians should acquiesce," writes Chernow. Her faith helped her to recover from the devastating loss and begin to imagine a new life.

Hamilton himself had encouraged her to remember her faith before his death. In his letter he wrote the night before his duel with Burr, he reminded Eliza, "The consolations of religion, my beloved, can alone support you and these you have a right to enjoy. Fly to the bosom of your God and be comforted. With my last idea, I shall cherish the sweet hope of meeting you in a better world."

As Eliza slowly recovered from her grief, she discovered a new calling. She partnered with a small group of women to found the first private orphanage in New York City. Her Hamilton had suffered as an orphan his entire life; now she would work to alleviate the suffering of others who faced the same struggle.

Orphans during this era faced a brutal reality, with no good options available to them. Many orphans lived on the streets in gangs, fighting a daily battle to survive. The tenement housing district was grossly overpopulated and overrun with abhorrent living conditions. Almshouses or indentured servitude provided shelter and food for a life of hard labor and a loss of freedom, but oftentimes created structures that abused vulnerable children.

For twenty-seven years, Eliza worked tirelessly, providing orphans a hopeful alternative. Chernow writes, "She oversaw every aspect of the orphanage work. She raised money, leased properties, visited almshouses, investigated complaints, and solicited donations of coal, shoes, and Bibles." Eliza believed that God himself had given her this calling, "My maker has pointed out this duty to me and has given me the ability and inclination to perform it."

The work challenged her greatly and oftentimes operated dangerously low on resources. Eliza once committed to never turning away a child, whether they possessed a dime in the treasury or not. In 1813, the orphanage account fell to $60 while caring for the needs of ninety children. Yet despite these ongoing challenges, Eliza believed in God's provision and faithfully continued her work. In doing so, she offered redemption to these children who otherwise faced a hopeless existence.

* * *

The end of Miranda's musical beautifully illustrates Eliza redeeming Hamilton's brokenness. The scene captures one of the most powerful artistic representations of redemption I've ever witnessed. The final song features Eliza singing about the different ways she honored her husband's legacy. She considered the orphanage her crowning achievement in this pursuit. She sings about how she helped hundreds of orphans in the city, and how she sees her husband in each child that she serves. The musical ends with a brilliant white spotlight shining on Eliza as she smiles, her face radiating joy as the theatre fades to black.

* * *

Eliza models our call as followers of Jesus. We are not simply to receive the promise of redemption for our own individual lives, although accepting that personal redemption is an important step. God also calls us also to partner with him in the ongoing task of redemption, of bringing his new creation to bear on this broken world.

N. T. Wright remarks, "We are called to be *part of* God's new creation, called to be *agents* of that new creation here and now. . . . [I]t is the new way of being human, the Jesus-shaped way of being human, the cross-and-resurrection way of life, the Spirit-led pathway. It is the way which anticipates, in the present, the full, rich, glad human existence which will one day be ours when God makes all things new."

* * *

The way we become "agents of that new creation here and now" is simple but hard: we love. Eliza made Hamilton's brokenness beautiful for hundreds of orphans by loving them in tangible ways. She threw herself into this work out of her love for her husband, and her love of God. Chernow writes, "Perhaps nothing expressed her affection for Hamilton more tenderly than her efforts on behalf of orphans. . . . Surely some extra dimension of religious fervor had entered into Eliza's feelings toward her husband because of his boyhood."

The work she pioneered continues to this day. The organization Eliza created more than two hundred years ago still exists, now called Graham Windham. The people of Graham Windham continue to live out Eliza's legacy, tirelessly working on behalf of poor children and families in New York City. The families they serve live in New York City's most severely distressed neighborhoods, ninety-five percent of whom live at or below the poverty line.

One woman, Joanna, experienced redemption with the help of the people at Graham Windham. She grew up with two addicts for parents, and she continued the cycle of addiction. "By twelve, I was sniffing cocaine, by thirteen I was smoking crack. I was pregnant by fourteen. I abandoned my kids, I left for two weeks, and when I came back, they were already in the system," she says.

Joanna connected with the people at Graham Windham, and the trajectory of her life changed. Her case worker said, "Joanna went through a lot, yet came out from it moving upward."

"Graham Windham is very supportive," Joanna says, "My worker has never come to my house and judged me. She helps me, empowers me, and supports me." Joanna, who lives again with her two children, is taking the broken pieces of her life and making them beautiful, redeeming her story in the process. She represents one of the many lives Graham Windham has transformed and redeemed.

Jess Dannhauser, the current president and CEO of Graham Windham, sees their work as a continuation of Eliza's legacy. Experiencing the musical *Hamilton* moved him deeply. "When Eliza sings that she sees Alexander in the eyes of these orphans, I see that as her saying these kids have great potential inside of them. That spirit is what animates our work today."

Kimberly Hardy Watson, Graham Windham's chief operating officer, agrees: "I find myself often wondering, what would Eliza think about what we are doing today? If she and the other cofounders had a clear understanding of what they endeavored for children, are we keeping to that promise? Are we being good stewards of that vision?" More than two hundred years after Eliza initiated this project, the brokenness continues to be made beautiful.

The cast of *Hamilton* participates in the work of Graham Windham. Some of the cast members participate as pen pals with children from Graham Windham. Phillipa Soo and Morgan Marcell created "The Eliza Project," with a mission to "use the arts as a means of expression, as an outlet for personal experience, and to uplift the creative spirit." Soo recruits other cast members to join her in teaching kids at Graham Windham acting, dance, and rap. These actors continue to tell Eliza's story of redemption, not only on the stage, but also in their tangible acts of love for these children.

* * *

Jean Vanier, founder of L'Arche communities, a group of homes that serve the mentally and physically handicapped, writes, "My experience has shown that when we welcome people from this world of anguish, brokenness, and depression, and when they gradually discover that they are wanted and loved as they are and that they have a place, then we witness a real transformation—I would even say 'resurrection.'" Author Marlena Graves responds to his words, "How beautiful. In Christ's power and through his presence, we can love others and be loved into resurrection. I have been loved into resurrection."

I love that phrase: loved into resurrection. I wonder how many orphans experienced that gift from Eliza? How many people have been loved into resurrection by the good people at Graham Windham? This phrase articulates precisely what Jesus has done for each of us. He looks at our lives and sees our failures and brokenness, but does not respond with judgment, impatience, or anger. Instead, he loves, forgives, and redeems. He offers grace upon grace upon grace.

We have been loved by Jesus into resurrection. His love makes all of our brokenness new. And now, because we have been loved into resurrection, he calls us to love others into that same reality. We do this by offering hope, forgiveness, empathy, and love to people who are overwhelmed by their brokenness, who can't even begin to imagine the possibility of redemption. We lead them gently into the truth that God's love is bigger than their brokenness.

We have the opportunity to share in Eliza's joy by joining in this project of redemption. N. T. Wright says, "We are called to *model* and *display* that new creation in symphonies and family life, in restorative justice and poetry, in holiness and service to the poor, in politics and painting." And maybe even in Broadway musicals.

Wright challenges us to model and display new creation, redemption from brokenness, in every single aspect of our lives. This challenge explains why the musical *Hamilton* continues to impact audiences across the nation. It models for us the story of redemption. And every time we experience that story, our souls come alive. The story of redemption inspires us to participate, to serve as agents of the new creation here and now. We all long to take the broken pieces we see all around us and by God's grace, make them beautiful.

Conclusion

The winter of 1777 at Valley Forge marked the low point in the Revolutionary War for Washington, Hamilton, and the entire Continental Army. Having lost two key battles and the strategic city of Philadelphia that fall, Washington's Army faced discouragement and despair as the winter approached. Washington selected Valley Forge, twenty miles northwest of Philadelphia, for their winter camp because of its obvious strategic advantages: it provided both safe distance from the British Army and close proximity to local agriculture, timber, and fresh water sources. As the winter began, Washington's army desperately needed a season to regroup and recuperate. Tragically, that winter would offer them little reprieve, ushering them into an unimaginable misery.

Washington's army faced every possible hardship that winter. Many died of starvation as extreme food shortages drove the men to desperate measures. Men baked a mixture of flour and water in iron kettles called "fire cakes," which were often infested by maggots and weevils. Many days men went without food at all, suffering extreme malnutrition. Other soldiers froze to death, lacking blankets, shoes, and proper clothing to protect themselves against the harsh winter elements. Due to frostbite, soldiers' legs and feet were routinely amputated. Crudely built log cabins with earth floors proved inadequate against the piercing winds and freezing temperatures. Disease, including typhus, influenza, and dysentery, ravaged the army as well. More than two thousand of Washington's eleven thousand men died that winter at Valley Forge.

Dr. Albigence Waldo of Connecticut described the scene, "Poor food—hard lodging—cold weather—fatigue—nasty clothes—nasty cookery—vomit half my time—smoke out of my senses—the devil's in it—I can't endure it. . . . There comes a soldier, his bare feet are seen through his worn-out shoes, his legs nearly naked from the tattered remains of an only pair of stockings; his breeches not sufficient to cover his nakedness; his shirt hanging in strings; his hair disheveled; his face meager; his whole appearance pictures a person forsaken and discouraged." In a desperate letter to Congress, Washington articulated the dire situation, "Unless some great change takes place, this army must inevitably starve, dissolve, or disperse."

With his army hanging by a thread, Washington approved an idea he hoped would encourage his troops and strengthen their resolve in the midst of the misery they faced. Soldiers arranged a production of his favorite play, *Cato,* which told the story of a Roman statesmen who gave his life in a battle against tyranny. I like to picture Hamilton, as Washington's aide-de-camp and administrative genius, helping direct or produce the play, although I admit I'm making quite an imaginative leap.

Washington understood that stories possess the power to transform. New Testament scholar William Willimon agrees, "A story not only means something but also *does* something."

This explains why Jesus relied on stories as his primary form of communication, "That's why I tell stories," Jesus says, "To create readiness, to nudge the people toward receptive insight."

Washington believed that art—in this case, theatre—could create new possibilities in his soldiers' minds and hearts. In the bleakest possible circumstances where men faced starvation, malnutrition, and brutal winter elements, Washington hoped a story about a man giving everything in his battle against tyranny might encourage and inspire his weary men for the battle against tyranny that lay before them.

* * *

This belief that stories possess the power to transform lies at the heart of Miranda's musical. McCarter writes, "We tell stories of people who are gone because like any powerful stories, they have the potential to inspire, and to change the world." Christopher Jackson encouraged the *Hamilton* cast with this idea during the prayer circle before each *Hamilton* performance. Each night when Jackson led that time of prayer, he shared the hope that everyone in the theatre might experience transformation. Jackson, and through him the cast of *Hamilton*, performed with a belief that Hamilton's story might actually change people's lives.

Thin places share this transformative power. Why else would God make the veil between heaven and earth translucent at times, if not to transform us? Paul articulates this reality: "God removes the veil and there they are—face-to-face! They suddenly recognize that God is a living, personal presence."

God gives us the gift of thin places, the gift of experiencing his presence and love in intimate ways, to aid us in his ultimate purpose for our lives: to be conformed to the image of Christ. This hope of transformation forms the core of the gospel. John Ortberg writes, "The Christian gospel insists that the transformation of the human personality really is possible. Never easy. Rarely quick. But possible."

Jesus and his three closest disciples, Peter, James, and John, experienced such a thin place on top of a mountaintop as his passion drew near. Up on the mountain, Jesus' face shone like the sun, he clothes became as white as the light, and Moses and Elijah appeared before them, talking with Jesus. The veil separating heaven and earth not only became thin, it disappeared altogether. This experience transformed the three disciples, as they saw Jesus in his heavenly glory. John Howard Yoder writes about how seeing Jesus in his glory and power transformed the disciples. Their experience "not only enables his disciples to face martyrdom when them must; it also enables his disciples to go about their daily crafts and trades, to do their duties as parents and neighbors, without being driven to despair by cosmic doubt."

I also like to believe that this moment transformed Jesus as well, not only physically but emotionally and spiritually. Not unlike in the garden of Gethsemane, when an angel came and strengthened him, this transfiguration experience must have encouraged and strengthened Jesus as he prepared to face his passion.

The story of Hamilton, experienced both through Miranda's musical and Chernow's biography, has transformed my life. I'll never forget certain moments from the musical: the forgiveness Eliza offered, the inner struggles of both Hamilton and Burr, the chaos from his affair with Maria Reynolds, the redemption Eliza offered that ended the production. Similarly, scenes from Chernow's book continue to resonate within me: Hamilton's ardent faith as a young boy, his passion and intensity in building this new nation, his final moments with his family on his deathbed. These moments inspire me to forgive, to be gentle with myself and my failures, to give my best efforts to the callings God gives me, and to pursue a life of authentic faith.

I hope that in reading this book, the intersection of these stories might transform you as well. Will you recognize the foundation of grace that God has established in your life? Can you find the courage to do battle with the shame that attacks your self-worth? Do you dare take initiative instead of giving into resistance? Will you welcome the outsider, accept forgiveness, forgive others, and practice the discipline of surrender? Will you partner with God is his project of bringing redemption to the entire creation?

* * *

During the early performances of *Hamilton* at the Public Theatre, Miranda met regularly with his team, which included Oskar Eustis, for script revisions. At these meetings, Eustis reminded Miranda of this truth: "characters define themselves through their choices." What is true of dramatic characters holds true in our lives as well. We define ourselves through the choices we make. I hope and pray the stories in this book influence your choices, the choices that define your very life. I pray that in some small way, these stories might transform you and lead you into the life that is truly life, the eternal life now, the life God offers to each and every one of us today.

Endnotes

Introduction

15. "*I have never in my*" "Hamilton's America," *Great Performances.* Directed by Alex Horwitz. PBS, 2016.

16. "*as form, not content. . . . [Hip-hop]*" Lin-Manuel Miranda and Jeremy McCarter, *Hamilton the Revolution* (New York: Grand Central Publishing, 2016), 10, 22.

16. "*You have no idea how*" Rebecca Mead, "All about the Hamiltons," *The New Yorker*, February 9, 2015, https://www.newyorker.com/magazine/2015/02/09/hamiltons.

17. "*the best piece of art*" "Hamilton's America." *Great Performances.*

17. "*the quintessential immigrant story, of*" Ibid.

17. "*By having a multicultural cast*" Mead.

18. "*Sometimes the right person tells*" Miranda and McCarter, 15.

19. "*a religious experience, a spiritual*" Ashley Lee, "Rosie O'Donnell Reflect on the Healing Power of 'Hamilton,' Which She's Seen 15 Times," *The Hollywood Reporter*, June 10, 2016, http://www.hollywoodreporter.com/news/rosie-odonnell-reflects-healing-power-901399.

19. "*I haven't felt this alive*" Mead.

20. *"overlap and interlock in a"* N. T. Wright, *Simply Christian* (San Francisco: Harper Collins, 2006), 63–64, 219.

20. *"Heaven . . . is a metaphor that"* Eugene Peterson, *Reversed Thunder* (San Francisco: Harper One, 1991), 169.

22. *"God saw all that he"* Genesis 1:31.

22. *"The arts are not the"* Wright, 235.

22. *"Shakespeare turns preacher,"* Frederick Buechner, *Telling the Truth: The Gospel and Tragedy, Comedy & Fairy Tale* (San Francisco: Harper San Francisco, 1977), 31.

22. *"And Shakespeare and all the"* Madeleine L'Engle, *Walking on Water: Reflections on Faith & Art* (New York: Convergent Books, 1980), 64.

22. *"I have more than once"* "Hamilton's America."

24. *"created the institutional scaffolding for"* Ron Chernow, *Alexander Hamilton* (New York: Penguin Group, 2004), 481.

24. *"We look in vain for"* Ibid., 481.

25. *"embodies the word's ability to make"* Miranda and McCarter, 225.

25. *"Theatre has an inherent spirituality"* Carey Purcell, "Chris Jackson Shares How Seeing Hamilton as a Child Would Have Changed Everything' For Him," *Playbill*, October 9, 2015, http://www.playbill.com/article/chris-jackson-shares-how-seeing-hamilton-as-a-child-would-have-changed-everything-for-him-com-366077.

26. *"He closes with the hope"* Miranda and McCarter, 59.

26. *In a keynote address that Miranda* John Moore, "Lin-Manuel Miranda on the power of theatre to eliminate distance," *DCPS Newsletter*, Denver Center for the Performing Arts, May 20, 2015, https://www.denvercenter.org/blog-posts/news-center/2015/05/20/lin-manuel-miranda-on-the-power-of-theatre-to-eliminate-distance.

Chapter 1: Grace

30. *"Their father had vanished,"* Chernow, 26.

30. *"Where now, oh! vile worm"* Ibid., 37.

31. *"Hamilton did not know it"* Ibid.

31. *Author Phillip Yancey tells a story* Philip Yancey, *What's So Amazing about Grace?* (Grand Rapids: Zondervan, 1997), 45.

32. *"Many years ago I was"* David Seamands, "Perfectionism: Fraught with Fruits of Self-Destruction," *Christianity Today*, April 10, 1981.

33. *"This letter, my very dear"* Chernow, 709.

34. *"my imagination wasn't (this) big."* Vahe Gregorian, "Bittersweet or Not, Frank Mason's Journey one to Celebrate," *Kansas City Star*, March 30, 2017, http://www.kansascity.com/sports/spt-columns-blogs/vahe-gregorian/article141861609.html.

35. *One of Jesus' most beloved* Luke 15:11–24.

36. *"Over and over again I"* Henri Nouwen, *The Return of the Prodigal Son: A Story of Homecoming* (New York: Doubleday, 1994), 39.

37. *"he seemed more skeptical about"* Chernow, 132.

39. *"If by grace,"* Paul writes Romans 11:6.

39. *"Grace means there is nothing"* Yancey, 70.

39. *"Grace teaches us that God"* Ibid., 280.

41. *suggests that in this act* Richard B. Vinson, *Luke: Smyth & Helwys Bible Commentary* (Macon, GA: Smyth & Helwys Publishing, 2006), 512.

41. *"But sin didn't, and doesn't"* Romans 5:20 (MSG).

43. *The grace that formed the foundation* McCarter, *Hamilton: The Revolution*, 157.

44. *"After one of the student performances"* Ibid.

44. *"entry reads, "Grace is everywhere."* Georges Bernanos, *The Diary of a Country Priest* (Boston: Da Capo Press, 2002), 298.

44. *see "through grace-tinted lenses."* Yancey, 272.

Chapter Two: Shame

47. *"wretched feelings of shame and"* Chernow, 40.

47. *"mass of insecurities that he"* Ibid., 144.

47. *"the hypersensitive boy from the"* Ibid., 309.

47. *"my birth is the subject"* Ibid., 8.

47. *"the bastard brat of a Scotch peddler"* Ibid., 522.

47. *published essays under the pen name* Ibid., 245.

48. *"Hamilton is a gone man."* Ibid., 129.

48. *"I am pleased with every"* Ibid., 149.

48. *"I know I have talents"* Ibid., 145.

49. *"I have not concealed my circumstances"* Joanne B. Freeman, *The Essential Hamilton: Letters and Other Writings* (New York: Library of America, 2017), 51– 52.

49. *"I'm sorry, I made a mistake."* Brene Brown, "Listening to Shame" [Video File], March 2012. Retrieved from https://www.ted.com/talks/brene_brown_listening_to_shame.

49. *"The feeling of shame is"* Lewis Smedes, *Shame & Grace: Healing the Shame We Don't Deserve* (New York: Harper Collins, 1993), 6.

50. *"A creature meant to be"* Ibid., 31.

50. *"Shame, we are told, is"* Ibid., 34.

51. *"Are they ashamed of their"* Jeremiah 8:12.

51. *"I say this to shame"* 1 Corinthians 6:5.

52. *"The producer of concerts made"* Smedes, 18.

52. *"I am disgusted with everything"* Chernow, 128.

53. *A U.S. News & World Report* Nirmala George, "For India's leprosy affected, stigma hinders efforts to fight

the disease," *U.S. News & World Report*, March 9, 2014, https://www.usnews.com/news/world/articles/2014/03/09/stigma-hinders-efforts-to-combat-leprosy-in-india.

53. *"Leprosy in Jesus' day was"* David A. Neale, *Luke 1–9, A Commentary in the Wesleyan Tradition*, New Beacon Bible Commentary (Kansas City, MO: Beacon Hill Press, 2013), 131.

54. *"His mother seated him apart"* Yancey, *What's So Amazing about Grace?*, 166.

54. *"Lord, if you are willing"* Luke 5:12.

55. *"There are few gestures as"* David Lose, "Four Words" *Working Preacher*, February 5, 2012, https://www.workingpreacher.org/craft.aspx?post=1561.

55. *"I am willing, be clean,"* Luke 5:13.

56. *"I was once determined to"* Miranda and McCarter, 107.

56. *"God made him who had"* 2 Corinthians 5:21.

57. *"Confess your sins to each"* James 5:16.

57. *"He who is alone with"* Dietrich Bonhoeffer, *Life Together: The Classic Exploration of Faith in Community* (New York: Harper Collins: 1954), 110.

57. *"Empathy," says Brene Brown in* Brown, "Listening to Shame."

Chapter Three: Faith

61. *"Hark! Hark! A voice from"* Nicole Scholet, "Poetry of Alexander Hamilton" *The AHA Society*, April 22, 2015, http://

the-aha-society.com/index.php/publications/articles/87-aha-society-articles/179-poetry-of-alexander-hamilton.

61. *"was attentive to public worship"* Chernow, 53.

62. *"Like the other founders and"* Ibid., 659.

62. *"The world has been scourged"* Ibid.

62. *"It is striking how religion"* Ibid.

62. *"experienced a resurgence of his"* Ibid., 660.

63. *"Without somehow destroying me in"* Frederick Buechner, cited at *Goodreads,* https://www.goodreads.com/quotes/320051-without-somehow-destroying-me-in-the-process-how-could-god.

64. *"The phone rang, and her"* John Ortberg, *Faith & Doubt* (Grand Rapids, MI: Zondervan, 2008), 19.

64. *"Doubt is not so much a"* Michael Novak, *Belief and Unbelief* (New Brunswick, NJ: Transaction, 2006), 7.

65. *In the Gospel of Mark* Mark 9:14–29.

67. *"Ban, delete, shred, obliterate the"* Karen Salmansohn, *Pinterest,* https://www.pinterest.com/pin/93942342199337092/.

67. *"This swagger, built on a"* Miranda and McCarter, 76.

68. *"Carry each other's burdens, and"* Galatians 6:2.

69. *"However loaded with superabundant talent"* Chernow, 144.

69. *"that showed him steeped in"* Ibid., 125.

70. *"What good is it, my"* James 2:14–17.

71. *"to be observed as a"* Michael Shea, *In God We Trust: George Washington and the Spiritual Destiny of the United States* (Derry, NH: Liberty Quest LLC, 2012), 74.

71. *"all officers, and soldiers, to"* "General Orders," *Founders Online,* https://founders.archives.gov/documents/Washington /03-04-02-0243.

71. *"Jesus has a very special"* David Van Biema, "Mother Teresa's Crisis of Faith," *Time,* August 23, 2007, http://time.com/4126238/mother-teresas-crisis-of-faith/.

Chapter Four: Initiative

73. *"These are the numbers that"* Miranda and McCarter, 21.

73. *"At present my time is"* Willard Sterne Randall, "Hamilton Takes Command," *Smithsonian,* January 2003, https://www.smithsonianmag.com/history/hamilton-takes-command-74722445/#84ut6JWFGrI8BRDb.99.

74. *"took charge of Washington's staff"* Chernow, 86.

74. *"the government established under the"* Joseph Ellis, *American Creation* (New York: Random House, 2007), 88.

75. *"Without some alteration in our"* Ibid., 91.

76. *"Hamilton surpassed all of his contemporaries"* James Kent, cited at *All Things Hamilton,* http://allthingshamilton.com/index.php/alexander-hamilton/thanks-to- alexander-hamilton/69-hamilton-s-greatest-hits/136-hgh-the-us-constitution.

77. *"Hamilton hit the ground running"* Chernow, 288.

77. *"If Washington was the father"* Ibid., 481.

77. *"Once Hamilton encountered a major"* Joseph Ellis, *Founding Brothers: The Revolutionary Generation* (New York: Random House, 2002), 60.

79. *"Everything David does is derivative"* Walter Brueggemann, *First and Second Samuel: Interpretation A Bible Commentary for Teaching and Preaching* (Louisville: Westminster John Knox Press, 1990), 132.

79. *"David takes no initiative. He"* Ibid., 140.

79. *"David is no longer a"* Ibid., 155, 202.

79. *When David enters the narrative* 1 Samuel 17.

80. *"the most toxic force on the"* Steven Pressfield, *The War of Art: Break through the Blocks and Win Your Inner Creative Battles* (New York: Black Irish Entertainment, 2012), Kindle ed. Location 68.

82. *"Burr is every bit as"* Mead.

83. *"But by the grace of"* 1 Corinthians 15:10.

84. *"Concerning all acts of initiative"* W. H. Murray, *The Scottish Himalayan Expedition*, quoted in Pressfield, 122.

85. *"Ten days more will put"* Chernow, 84.

85. *"great turning point"* in David McCullough, *1776* (New York: Simon & Schuster Paperbacks, 2005), 290.

85. *"The two late actions at"* Ibid.

Chapter Five: The Outsider

87. *"the most radical and important"* Gordon Wood, *Revolutionary Characters: What Made the Founders Different* (New York: Penguin Press, 2006), 209.

87. *"These are the times that"* Thomas Paine, http://www.ushistory.org/paine/crisis/c-01.htm.

88. *"He chose a psychological strategy"* Chernow, 40, 59.

88. *"No immigrant in American history"* Ibid., 406.

88. *"bastard brat of a Scotch peddler,"* Ibid., 522.

88. *"could scarcely acquire the opinions"* Ibid.

89. *"a more careful and attentive"* Ibid., 571.

89. *"People would assume that Hamilton"* Ibid., 124.

93. *"I'm here to invite outsiders"* Matthew 9:13 (MSG).

93. *"The spirit of Jesus penetrates"* Donald Kraybill, *The Upside Down Kingdom* (Scottsdale, PA: Herald Press, 1978), 224.

94. *"When a foreigner resides among"* Leviticus 19:34.

94. *"Holiness must be manifest in"* Samuel E. Balentine, *Leviticus: Interpretation: A Bible Commentary for Teaching and Preaching* (Louisville: Westminster John Knox Press, 2011), 160.

94. *"Love is a mighty power"* Thomas a Kempis, *Imitation of Christ* (New York: Random House, 1955), 97.

95. *"As for you, you were"* Ephesians 2:1–2, 4–5.

96. *"were both foreigners and therefore"* Chernow, 477.

96. *"Findley, who had been born"* Ibid., 477.

96. Later, Hamilton *"predicted that 'the'"* Ibid., 658.

97. *"The church has always been"* Ann Voskamp, "Known by Our Gratitude," Q Conference, May 2017.

98. *"What I found,"* writes Jo" J. D. Payne, *Strangers Next Door: Immigration, Migration and Mission* (Downers Grove, IL: InterVarsity Press, 2012), 25.

98. *Fatima arrived five years ago* Ibid.

98. *"Taking classes in a different"* Ibid., 26.

99. *"I am a stranger in"* Chernow, 150.

100. *Miranda and his team decided* Miranda and McCarter, 121.

Chapter Six: Sinner and Saint

103. *"an American prophet without peer,"* Chernow, 344.

103. *"I need not add that"* Ibid., 502.

104. *"Hamilton wrote dozens of such tender"* Ibid., 502.

104. *"was deep and constant if"* Ibid., 367.

104. *"What kind of a guy"* Hamilton's America." *Great Performances*. PBS. 2016.

104. *"His inability to shut up"* Ibid.

104. *"Charming and impetuous, romantic and"* Chernow, 5.

105. *"the greatest generation of political"* Ellis, *Founding Brothers*, 13.

105. *"British philosopher Alfred North Whitehead"* Ibid., 16.

106. *"The darkest shadow is unquestionably"* Ellis, *American Creation*, 10.

106. *"descending a staircase with our"* Miranda and McCarter, 152.

106. *"Washington, bows his head in"* Ibid., 208.

106. *"There were great things that"* "Hamilton's America."

106. *"These are not perfect people"* Ibid.

107. *"Our show does a good"* Ibid.

107. *"Taken together, these triumphal and"* Ellis, 11.

107. *"The test of a first-rate"* F. Scott Fitzgerald, Cited from *Wikiquote*, https://en.wikiquote.org/wiki/Talk:F._Scott_Fitzgerald.

108. *"Peter's character, as presented in"* George Lyons, *Galatians: A Commentary in the Wesleyan Tradition*, (Kansas City, MO: Beacon Hill Press, 2012), 140.

108. *"Take courage! It is I."* Matthew 14:22–32.

109. *"You are the Messiah, the"* Matthew 16:13–23.

109. *"Even if all fall away"* Matthew 26:31–35.

109. *life exhibits a "jarring juxtaposition."* W. D. Davies and Dale C. Allison, Jr., *A Critical and Exegetical Commentary on the Gospel According to Saint Matthew*, 2 Vols. (Edinburgh: T. & T. Clark, 1988–91), 2:665.

110. *"Jesus tells a story about"* Luke 18:9–14.

110. *"Though, in reviewing the incidents"* George Washington, cited at https://www.gpo.gov/fdsys/pkg/GPO-CDOC-106sdoc21/pdf/GPO-CDOC-106sdoc21.pdf.

111. *"In [his farewell address], Washington"* Miranda and McCarter, 210.

111. *"Is the flawed, historically accurate"* Ibid., 125.

111. *"[Hamilton's flaws] allow the audience"* Ibid., 126.

111. *"new discoveries, new mistakes"* became Ibid., 206.

112. *"I am not a saint,"* Nelson Mandela, Cited at *Goodreads*, https://www.goodreads.com quotes/40281-i-am-not-a-saint -unless-you-think-of-a.

112. *"A saint is not someone"* Thomas Merton, Cited at *Goodreads*, https://www.goodreads.com/quotes/495841-when-i-get-honest-i-admit-i-am-a-bundle.

113. *"For we are God's masterpiece."* Ephesians 2:10 (NLT).

113. *"Our job is to remind people"* Richard Rohr, Cited at *If Grace Is an Ocean We Are All Drowning*, https://ifgrace-isanoceanwerealldrowning.wordpress.com/2014/   12/30/ our-job-is-to-remind-people-of-their-inherent-goodness-richard-rohr.

114. *"Character mattered because the fate"* Ellis, *Founding Brothers*, 47.

114. *"a realistic response to the"* Ibid., 46.

114. *"Burr, if I have him right"* Ibid., 18.

115. *"I will always be staggering"* Flannery O'Connor, *A Prayer Journal* (New York: Farrar, Straus and Giroux, 2013), 22.

116. *"Dear God," she writes, "I"* Ibid., 3.

116. *"Mass again . . . has left me"* Ibid., 35.

116. *"My thoughts are so far"* Ibid., 40.

116. *"Please help me to get"* Ibid., 4.

116. *"I want so to love"* Ibid., 23.

116. *"I don't want to be"* Ibid., 35.

116. *"It's so important to take"* Miranda, "Hamilton's America."

Chapter Seven: Equality

119. *"Chief among a woman's truths"* Carol Berkin, *Revolutionary Mothers* (New York: Random House, 2005), 4.

119. *"The lingering belief that the"* Ibid., 5.

120. *"[I am] making it the"* Ibid., 9.

120. *"only motive was a sense"* Ibid., 68.

120. *"When we're introduced to Hamilton's"* Emma Miller, "Here's Why Every Feminist (and Person) Need to See 'Hamilton,'" *HelloFlo*, January 8, 2016, http://helloflo.com/heres-why-every-feminist-needs-to-see-hamilton.

121. *"It always seemed a most"* James Oliver Horton, "Alexander Hamilton: Slavery and Race in a Revolutionary Generation," *The New York Journal of American History, Issue 3* (2004).

Retrieved from   http://www.alexanderhamiltonexhibition. org/about/Horton%20-%20Hamiltsvery_Race.pdf.

121. *"[Hamilton] was one of those"* Ibid.

121. *"for their natural faculties are"* Ibid.

121. *"By having a multi-cultural cast"* Mead.

122. *Paul confronted Peter on this* Galatians 2:11–21.

123. *"It's hard for Westerners today"* N. T. Wright, *Paul For Everyone: Galatians and Thessalonians* (Louisville: Westminster John Knox Press, 2004), 21, 32.

123. *"Shared meals demonstrated mutual trust"* George Lyons, *Galatians: A Commentary in the Wesleyan Tradition*, NBBC (Kansas City, MO: Beacon Hill Press, 2012), 132.

123. *"Jewish zealots threatened violence"* Ibid., 128.

124. *"So in Christ Jesus you"* Galatians 3:26–28.

124. *"Blessed be God that he"* Scot McKnight, *Galatians: The NIV Application Commentary* (Grand Rapids: Zondervan, 1995), 200.

124. *"It's difficult for us to"* Kraybill, *Upside Down Kingdom*, 214.

125. *"If the church is to"* Richard Hays, *The New Interpreter's Bible*, (Nashville: Abingdon Press, 2000), 273.

125. *"[This passage announces] the irrelevancy"* McKnight, 201.

125. *"constantly assimilating, till they embrace"* Miranda and McCarter, 88.

126. *"acknowledged that Paul's idealistic vision"* Lyons, 235.

126. *"Women were talked about in"* McKnight, 202.

126. *Makers.com, a platform fighting for* Makers team, "21 Facts You Never Knew About International Gender Inequality," *Makers,* March 7, 2015. https://www.makers.com/blog/21-facts-you-never-knew-about-international-gender-inequality.

127. *"In the U.S., my female"* Lyons, 140–141.

127. *"[Jesus'] treatment of women implies"* Kraybill, 215.

128. *"J. C. Nichols didn't sell houses"* Tanner Colby, *Some of My Best Friends Are Black: The Story of Integration in America* (New York: Penguin Books, 2012), 90.

128. *"None of said land may"* Ibid., 91.

128. *"colored parishioners typically sat in"* Ibid., 235.

129. *"Upon seeing a black man"* Ibid., 226.

129. *"stopped him cold," and reminded* Miranda and McCarter, 208.

130. *"He savaged Catholics and Protestants"* Colby, 244.

130. *"For he himself is our peace"* Ephesians 2:14–15.

131. *"A whole lot of things"* Miranda and McCarter, 149.

131. *Bill Coulter, a teacher from* Ibid., 159.

132. *"In 1994 [in Rwanda], members"* Richard Hays, "Galatians," 11:248, from E. Thomas, "Can These Bones Live?"

SOMA (Sharing of Ministries Abroad) *Newsletter* (Oct 15, 1996): 1–15.

Chapter Eight: Forgiveness

133. *"who for a long time"* Chernow, 364.

134. *"one of history's most mystifying"* Ibid., 362.

134. *"Once Callender's charges were published"* Ibid., 532.

135. *"incapable of a wise silence,"* Ibid., 534.

135. *"The charge against me is"* Ibid., 533.

135. *"Alas, alas, how weak is"* Ibid., 536.

135. *"Indeed my angelic Betsey, I"* Freeman, *The Essential Hamilton*, 71.

136. *"Author and historian Tilar Mazzeo"* Tilar Mazzeo, in discussion with the author, June 2017.

136. *Psalm 130 articulates this desperate* Psalm 130:1–8.

137. *"discerns the human situation. Life"* James Luther Mays, *Interpretation: Psalms* (Louisville: John Knox Press), 406.

137. *"It is not just guilt,"* Ibid.

138. *"[Hamilton] reiterated his faith in"* Chernow, 418.

138. *Miranda's team captured this chaos* Miranda and McCarter, 228.

139. *"the prayer is an act"* Walter Brueggemann, *The Message of the Psalms* (Minneapolis, Augsburg Publishing House, 1984), 104.

140. *"Does God forgive us because"* Lewis Smedes, *The Art of Forgiving: When You Need to Forgive and Don't Know How* (New York: Ballantine Books, 1996), 66.

141. *In Jesus' parable of the* Matthew 18:21–35.

142. *"Forgiveness," Phillip Yancey says, "is"* Yancey, 84.

142. *"Everyone says forgiveness is a"* C. S. Lewis, *Mere Christianity*, cited at *Goodreads,* https://www.goodreads.com/quotes/198171-everyone-thinks-forgiveness-is-a-lovely-idea-until-he-has.

142. *Phillipa Soo, who played Eliza* Miranda and McCarter, 228.

143. *"I've heard it all my"* Smedes, 4.

143. *"I could hardly breathe," writes* Hillary Clinton, "In Book, Hillary Clinton Details Pain from Monika Lewinsky Affair," *The New York Times,* June 4, 2003, http://www.nytimes.com/2003/06/04/us/in-book-hillary-clinton-details-pain-from-lewinsky-affair.html.

144. *"The most common Greek word"* Yancey, 96.

144. *"The first and often the"* Smedes, *Shame and Grace,* 136, 141.

144. *"Author Tilar Mazzeo points out"* Mazzeo, in discussion with the author, June 2017.

Chapter Nine: Despair

147. *"I am not worth exceeding"* Chernow, 483.

148. *"Once Jefferson became president, Hamilton"* Ibid., 640.

149. *"Hamilton regarded Philip as the"* Ibid., 651.

149. *"Just as most duels in"* Ellis, *Founding Brothers*, 35.

150. *"Having been abandoned by his"* Chernow, 655.

150. *"Eliza was inconsolable. . . . Angelica"* Ibid., 654–655.

150. *"Never did I see a"* Ibid, 655.

152. *"The way that the 19"* Miranda and McCarter, 135.

152. *"My tears have been my"* Psalm 42:5–11.

154. *"I believe I may, with"* McCullough, 110.

154. *"Oh how I feel for"* Ibid., 255.

154. *"We must bear up against"* Ibid., 256.

154. *"I will not however despair."* Ibid.

155. *"We must talk to ourselves"* D. Martyn Lloyd-Jones, *Spiritual Depression: Its Causes and Cure* (Grand Rapids, MI: Eerdmans Publishing Company, 1965), 20.

155. *"Instead of allowing this self"* Ibid., 21.

156. *"We all talk to ourselves"* Christopher P. Neck, Charles C. Manz, Jeffery D. Houghton, *Self-Leadership: The Definitive Guide to Personal Excellence* (Los Angeles: SAGE Publications, 2016), 94.

156. *"Luther had no trouble in"* Mark D. Thompson, "Luther on Despair," 12, http://www.academia.edu/7250610/Luther_on_Despair.

157. *"state in which hope despairs"* James Luther Mays, *Preaching and Teaching the Psalms* (Louisville: Westminster John Knox Press, 2006), 116.

157. *"Spirituality is about seeing . . . once"* Richard Rohr, *Everything Belongs* (New York: Crossroad Publishing, 1999), 33–34.

158. *"We can't leap over our"* Ibid., 46–47.

158. *"And we know that in"* Romans 8:28.

Chapter Ten: Surrender

161. *"While all other passions decline"* Chernow, 641.

161. *"[Hamilton] surprises [Eliza] with the"* Mazzeo, in discussion with the author, June 2017.

162. *"He even communicated a political"* Chernow, 643.

162. *"A garden, you know, is"* Alexander Hamilton, Wall text, Hamilton Grange National Memorial, Harlem, New York.

163. *"Washington's decision to forgo a"* Chernow, 505.

163. *"the entire [document] had the"* Chernow, *Washington: A Life* (New York: Penguin Books, 2010), 443.

163. *"that he would most graciously"* George Washington, cited at George Washington's Mount Vernon, http://www.mountvernon.org/george-washington/quotes/article/i-now-make-it-my-earnest-prayer-that-god-would-have-you-and-the-state-over-which-you-preside-in-his-holy-protection-that-he-would-incline-the-hearts-of-the-citizens-to-cultivate-a-spirit-of-subordination-and-obedience-to-government-to-entertain-a-brotherl/.

164. *"If he does that, he"* George Washington, cited at https://www.cato.org/publications/commentary/man-who-would-not-be-king.

164. *"depth and scope and sterling"* Chernow, 506.

164. *"Surrender yourself to the Lord"* Psalm 37:7 (GW).

165. *"born to hopes and prayers."* Ann Voskamp, *One Thousand Gifts* (Grand Rapids: Zondervan, 2011), 20.

166. *"Whoever makes a habit of"* Fr. Jean Baptiste Saint-Jure, S.J. and St. Claude de la Colombiere, S.J., *Trustful Surrender to Divine Providence: The Secret of Peace and Happiness* (Charlotte, NC: Tan Books, 1980), 29, 30.

166. *"Once I wrote this passage"* Miranda and McCarter, 120.

166. *The Garden of Gethsemane offers* Mark 14:32–35.

166. *"the watershed [moment] in the"* Joel Green, *The Gospel of Luke* (Grand Rapids, MI: William B. Eerdmans Publishing Company, 1997), 777.

167. *First, ripe olives would be* Ray Vander Laan, "Gethsemane and the Garden Press," *That The World May Know*, https://www.thattheworldmayknow.com/gethsemane-and-the-olive-press.

168. *"Jesus was like a man"* N. T. Wright, *New Testament Prayer for Everyone* (London: SPCK Publishing, 2012), 47.

169. *"[Hamilton] instantly turned from the"* Chernow, 653.

169. *"It was the will of"* Ibid., 655–656.

170. *"Trust in the Lord with"* Proverbs 3:5–6.

171. *"Well, even with our boys"* Voskamp, 21.

171. *"For I have come down"* John 6:38.

171. *"frequent practice of the virtue"* Colombiere, 95–96.

173. *"I have resolved, if our"* Ellis, *Founding Brothers*, 23.

174. *"It is the effect of"* Alexander Hamilton, cited at https://founders.archives.gov/documents/Hamilton/01-26-02-0001-0241.

174. *"But you had rather I"* Chernow, 697.

Chapter Eleven: Death

175. *In many towns, church bells* "From Cherubs to Cryonics: The Mindset List® of American Death and Remembrance," Legacy.com, http://www.legacy.com/life-and-death/the-liberty-era.html.

175. *"face [that had been] strongly"* Chernow, 656.

176. *"Of all things that move"* Ernest Becker, *The Denial of Death* (New York: Simon & Schuster Inc., 1973), 11, 15.

177. *"countless unnoticed, forgotten, and smaller"* Michael Pasquarello III, *Feasting on the Word: Year C, Volume 2, Lent through Eastertide* (Louisville: Westminster John Knox Press, 2010), 465.

177. *"There is nothing you can"* Miranda and McCarter, 252.

177. *"Every line of 'Quiet Uptown'"* Michael Paulson, "Hamilton and Heartache: Living the Unimaginable," *The New York Times*, Oct. 13, 2016, https://www.nytimes.com/2016/10/16/theater/oskar-eustis-public-theater.html.

178. *"In the hours that followed"* Jerry Sittser, A *Grace Disguised: How the Soul Grows through Loss* (Grand Rapids, MI: Zondervan, 1995), 26.

178. *"I visited the funeral home"* Ibid., 41.

178. *"Loss reminds us that we"* Ibid., 164.

179. *"a culmination of long-standing personal"* Ellis, *Founding Brothers*, 32.

179. *"his wife almost frantic with"* Chernow, 708.

180. *"he opened his eyes, gave"* Ibid.

180. *"My God, my God, why"* Matthew 27:46.

181. *begins with "At that moment."* Matthew 27:51.

183. *David writes, "My God, my"* Psalm 22:1–2, 12–13, 16.

183. *"I will declare your name"* Psalm 22:22–24.

184. *"At the same moment and"* 1 Corinthians 15:53–56 (MSG).

185. *"Hamilton was preoccupied with spiritual"* Chernow, 706.

185. *"Mason tried to console Hamilton"* Ibid., 707.

186. *"Cancer has kicked down the"* Kate Bowler, "Death, the Prosperity Gospel, and Me," *The New York Times*, Feb 13, 2016, https://www.nytimes.com/2016/02/14/opinion/sunday/death-the-prosperity-gospel-and-me.html.

187. *"Gifts of grace come to"* Sittser, 79.

187. *"Jesus had been killed, had"* Ibid., 167.

187. *"Remember, my Eliza, you are"* Chernow, 706.

Chapter 12: Redemption

190. *an article written by an orphan* David Divine, "Growing Up in an Orphanage: Tales of Personal Resilience," *Institute of Hazard, Risk, and Resilience Blog*, July 3, 2013, http://ihrrblog.org/2013/07/03/growing-up-in-an-orphanage-a-tale-of-personal-resilience.

190. *Another girl whose parents died* https://www.quora.com/What-is-it-like-to-grow-up-an-orphan.

191. *"To be human is to"* R. M. Drake, cited at *Goodreads*, https://www.goodreads.com/quotes/1146812-to-be-human-is-to-be-broken-and-broken-is. Used with permission from the author.

191. *"And she always had a"* R. M. Drake, cited at *Goodreads*, https://www.goodreads.com/quotes/4108077-and-she-always-had-a-way-with-her-brokenness-she. Used with permission from the author.

192. *"For Eliza Hamilton, the collapse"* Chernow, 723.

192. *"burst into tears, told him"* Ibid., 709.

193. *"Then I saw 'a new"* Revelation 21:1–2, 5.

194. *"The biblical story began, quite"* Peterson, *Feasting on the Word*, 467.

194. *The characters in Jesus' resurrection* John 20–21.

195. *"Suffering from the 'irreparable loss"* Chernow, 723.

196. *"The consolations of religion, my"* Ibid., 709.

196. *"She oversaw every aspect of"* Ibid., 728–729.

198. *"We are called to be"* Wright, *Simply Christian*, 236, 222.

198. *"Perhaps nothing expressed her affection"* Chernow, 728.

199. *"By twelve, I was sniffing"* Graham Windham, "Graham Windham's Impact in Action," YouTube video, 6:07, posted 2013, https://www.youtube.com/watch?v=ekwt0Gum UnI&t=253s.

200. *"The Eliza Project," with a* Michael Dale, "Hamilton's Phillipa Soo Extends Her Character's Charitable Legacy With 'The Eliza Project,'" *Broadway World*, December 30, 2015, https://www.broadwayworld.com/article/HAMILTONs-Phillipa-Soo-Extends-Her-Characters-Charitable-Legacy-With-The-Eliza-Project-20151230.

200. *"My experience has shown that"* Jean Vanier, cited in Marlena Graves, *A Beautiful Disaster: Finding Hope in the Midst of Brokenness* (Grand Rapids, MI: Brazos Press, 2014), 50.

201. *"We are called to model"* Wright, 236.

Conclusion

203. *iron kettles called "fire cakes,"* Chernow, *Washington: A Life*, 325.

203. *Many days men went without* Stephanie Butler, "Starving Soldiers at Valley Forge," *History.com*, September 27, 2013, http://www.history.com/news/hungry-history/starving-soldiers-at-valley-forge.

204. *"Poor food—hard lodging—cold"* Chernow, *Washington: A Life,* 325.

204. *"Unless some great change takes"* James A. Crutchfield, *George Washington: First in War, First in Peace* (New Word City ebooks), 101.

204. *"A story not only means"* William Willimon, *Acts: Interpretation: A Bible Commentary for Teaching and Preaching* (Atlanta: John Knox Press, 2010), 2.

205. *"That's why I tell stories,"* Matthew 13:12 (MSG).

205. *"We tell stories of people"* Miranda and McCarter, 277.

205. *"God removes the veil and"* 2 Corinthians 3:16–18 (MSG).

206. *"The Christian gospel insists that"* John Ortberg, *The Life You've Always Wanted: Spiritual Disciplines for Ordinary People* (Grand Rapids, MI: Zondervan, 1997), 9.

206. *"not only enables his disciples"* John Howard Yoder, *The Priestly Kingdom: Social Ethics as Gospel* (Notre Dame, IN: University of Notre Dame Press, 1984), 61.

207. *"characters define themselves through their"* Miranda and McCarter, 271.

Contact the Author

GodandHamilton.com
Facebook.com/GodandHamilton
Twitter: @kevincloudkc
Facebook.com/kevincloudkc

Like this book? Share it with your friends!
Share the book on your social media platforms. Use the hashtag #GodandHamilton.
Write a book review on your blog.
Share this message on Twitter or Facebook: "I loved #GodandHamilton by @kevincloudkc."

5% of the author's proceeds will be donated to

Graham Windham,

the organization Eliza Hamilton created
to serve orphans in
New York City over 200 years ago.

For more information about Graham Windham,
visit their website at:
http://www.graham-windham.org